EDUCATION FOR THE TELEVISION AGE

The Proceedings of a
National Conference on the
Subject of Children and Television

Conference Directors and Editors

MILTON E. PLOGHOFT

*Ohio University
Athens, Ohio*

and

JAMES A. ANDERSON

*University of Utah
Salt Lake City, Utah*

CHARLES C THOMAS • PUBLISHER
Springfield • Illinois • U.S.A.

Published and Distributed Throughout the World by
CHARLES C THOMAS • PUBLISHER
2600 South First Street
Springfield, Illinois, 62717, U.S.A.

This book is protected by copyright. No part of it
may be reproduced in any manner without written
permission from the publisher.

© 1981 *by* CHARLES C THOMAS • PUBLISHER
ISBN 0-398-04615-8
Library of Congress Catalog Card Number: 81-52760

With *THOMAS BOOKS careful attention is given to all details of manufacturing and design. It is the Publisher's desire to present books that are satisfactory as to their physical qualities and artistic possibilities and appropriate for their particular use. THOMAS BOOKS will be true to those laws of quality that assure a good name and good will.*

Printed in the United States of America
I-RX-1

LIBRARY OF CONGRESS
CATALOG CARD NO.: 81-52760

Ploghoft, Milton E., & James A. Anderson
Education for the television age.

Springfield, IL : Thomas, Charles C, Pub.
184 p.
8111   810721

Foreword

The first national conference to deal with the topic, Children and Television: Implications for Education, was held from November 4-7, 1979 in Philadelphia. Academicians, teachers, school administrators, parents, television industry specialists, and government agency personnel were broadly represented in the Conference. Participants came from more than 30 states and 5 foreign nations.

The proceedings which are included in this publication report on the plenary sessions which, with minor exceptions, follow the sequence of the Conference sessions. There were four presentations for which papers were not available for inclusion here.

Discussion opportunities called Analysis and Reaction Sessions were important features of the Conference. The flavor and highlights of these discussions are included to the extent possible. Much of the value of the Conference was realized in the give and take of such discussions.

This second printing of the conference papers makes available a source of comprehensive information on the important subject of education for the television age. It is intended as an authoritative reference for educators, parents and others concerned with the welfare of children and the educational programs that are provided for them.

Table of Contents

Section		
I.	Television and Education: Prologue and Overview	7
	Television as Popular Culture - Horace Newcomb	9
	Receivership Skills: An Educational Response - James A. Anderson	19
	The Child as Viewer - Ellen Wartella	28
	Support for a Skillful Audience - Donald E. Agostino	35
	Beyond 1984 - Peggy Charren	42
	A Legislator's Perspective - The Honorable Marc Lincoln Marks	48
II.	Elementary Viewing Skills Projects	53
	The Way We See It In Idaho Falls - Craig Ashton	55
	A Public Station Reaches Out - Debbi Bilowit	64
	Critical Viewing for Young Children - Dorothy G. Singer	71
III.	Secondary Viewing Skill Projects	83
	The East Syracuse Program - Suzanne Schaff	85
	The Eugene, Oregon Project - Melva Ellingsen	88
	The Far West Laboratory Project - Donna Lloyd-Kolkin	91
IV.	Network and Association Activities	99
	Educational Projects at ABC - Pamela Warford	101
	N.E.A. and Receivership Skills Curriculum - Karen Klass	106
	The P.T.A. Project - Marion R. Young	111
	What the TV Industry is Doing - Jack Blessington	116
V.	The Environment of Educational Innovation	123
	Critical Viewing Skills and the Basics - Milton E. Ploghoft	125
	Innovation at the District Level - James F. Parsley	132
	The Role of Teacher Education - Bob G. Woods	139
	Pitfalls and Pathways to change - Fritz Hess	149
VI.	Intended Effects of Critical Viewing Skills Curriculum	155
	Effects on Advertising Forms - Seymour Banks	157
	Social Uses of Television - James T. Lull	164
	Education for the Age of Television - George Gerbner	173

SECTION I

Television and Education:
Prologue and Overview

Receivership skills as this section of the conference proceedings will develop refer to those skills for the assimilation and utilization of information for some purposeful action. They involve the collection, interpretation, testing and application of information regardless of medium of presentation. The notion of receivership skills conceptualizes the individual as a consumer of information. As a knowledgeable consumer the individual has need of common skills of analysis (as in critical thinking) medium specific skills of reception and interpretation (as in critical reading for print materials) and content specific skills of understanding (as in the traditional rubric of criticism).

The first two papers in this section develop the two perspectives from which receivership skills are usually approached. The first, presented by Newcomb, adopts the study of media as an index of who we are as a people belonging to a common culture. Newcomb notes that culture--that set of shared values, rules of behaving and common symbols for understanding the world around us--is in a continual process negotiation. That negotiation gets done in the clubrooms of the rotaries, in the halls of churches, and in the expression of the media. The contemporary content of our media provides the panapoly of issues, problems, conflicts, offers and counter offers which the current negotiations involve. The content of our media is not trivial, therefore, but is composed of the shared values, ideas and symbols by which we survive as a people.

Anderson develops the second perspective: The media form a utility, the use and influence of which must be managed by each individual. As with the resources of any utility there is consumer management that is wasteful and inefficient and that which will return benefit to the community at large. This perspective is directed toward the pragmatics of social process, toward the social consequences of media in everyday life by considering the individual motives, uses and consequences.

All curricula require an understanding of the student audience. Wartella provides that overview of the child as viewer tracing the major epochs of attendance and understanding from earliest viewing to adult.

In the fourth paper Agostino explores the symbiotic relationship among parents, schools, consumer groups, and the television industry which is necessary for and a consequence of the formation of a skillful audience. In a provocative conclusion, he outlines five major abjectives for these four groups in order to provide media content appropriate to such an audience.

Television As Popular Culture:
Toward A Critically Based Curriculum

Horace Newcomb

INTRODUCTION

For many, a serious study of the content of popular culture in terms other than as a social problem is the study of trivia. Another criticism is that all such study is an attempt to rescue that trivia from a well deserved state of social disrespect. These are minor criticisms, faced immediately and effectively by any teacher of popular culture on the first day of class when a large group of students must be disabused of the notion that they are gathered in a course which will "groove on comic books" or remember with weepy nostalgia that Beaver Cleaver's mother always wore earrings and a necklace while cooking breakfast.

The more serious charge is that popular culture studies actually have nothing of substance to contribute to discussions such as this one in which real life issues are at stake, that they remain isolated in the mildly interesting, but socially and scientifically unrelated realm of formal aesthetic analysis. I hope that my comments today will serve as a demonstration that this is not the case. At the same time, any honest response must admit some truth in all the criticisms I've mentioned. But no more truth is there, I would argue, than is found in criticism of other approaches to television. No one of us has

---

Horace Newcomb, Ph.D. is Associate Professor of English at the University of Texas-Austin.

the answers locked up, and it is dialogue and exchange that we are after here. All pursuits of knowledge can be conducted well or poorly, and at all levels from preschool to post-doctoral. It is in hopes of avoiding any possibility of incorporating weaknesses into materials designed for younger students of television that I added to the title of my comments and refer to them as: "Television As Popular Culture: Toward A Critically Based Curriculum." The operative concepts in this expanded Title are *culture* and *criticism*. It is from their interaction, particularly the operation of criticism on culture that new, rich, complex approaches to television are emerging almost daily.

THE STUDY OF TELEVISION IN A CULTURAL CONTEXT

We can begin, then, by reinstating television within a cultural context. In doing so we immediately remove ourselves from the bind of unnecessary hierarchies. The term "popular" should not be used, certainly at the outset, as an immediate sign of inferiority. While we will almost certainly wish to return later to qualitative distinctions, it would be most unwise—certainly uncritical—to begin our study and design on the assumption that television is an inherently inferior medium or artistic expression or entertainment. Neither the technical capabilities nor the current organizational patterns of television lead to that conclusion. It would be an unwise assertion because it could hardly be supported and there is no need to back ourselves into rhetorical corners from the beginning. It would be uncritical because it would be to repeat the mistakes made with certain forms of drama, with printing presses, novels, newspapers, films, automobiles, comics and radio. It would be nice to *prove* that something, anything, is all bad, is inherently inferior prior to human use, if for no other reason than to validate some of our past errors and to absolve human beings from clear responsibilities, but it just won't work that way.

The cultural context, then, forces us to look at television as used by people in history. We must consider the history of technologies and developments of media. Generally this consideration will moderate our sweeping generalizations about how technologies shape the texture of our lives. Elizabeth Eisenstein's (2) recent study of the influences of the printing press on western culture is a marvelous example of such moderation.

More specifically we will have to understand the role of entertainment in culture and society and become more aware of the history of entertainment forms and content. Crucial to this process is a clearer analysis of our social responses to these forms. In this area we face, as I indicated earlier, the puzzling tendency to make scapegoats of all new media, scapegoats on which we hang all of society's ills. This is not meant to indicate that television is not fundamentally different from other technologies and other entertainment media. But whatever differences there may be can in no way remove our responsibility for understanding television's cultural and historical relationships.

Essentially, however, these first questions are background matters. While we would expect any teacher of television studies to have been instructed in these areas, it is doubtful that they would be immediately central to lower level work for students. Far more fundamental to practical classroom work is the content of television. It is here that we must focus our cultural analysis.

TELEVISION AS A FOCUS FOR CULTURAL ANALYSIS

The best definitions of culture that we have are those which see it as a system of shared meanings and values expressed through symbols. We are a culture to the extent that we share basic assumptions about the nature of life, of what is good, what is appropriate. Such a view of culture is in no way static, uniform, or unchanging. We know that there are deep rifts in the surface of all cultures, most often expressed in the form of social anxiety, debate, argument. Sometimes such conflict results in private violation of the norms, sometimes in political change, sometimes in more violent upheaval. Culture, then, while centered on shared symbols, is essentially a *process*. We are constantly negotiating new meanings, including new models of the good and the acceptable. We redefine our sense of self and other, of purpose and means. We create new symbolic expressions of these changes, most often by combining old symbols into new statements. In these cases the residue of old meanings is never totally removed from the new value. There is ceaseless shift and overlap.

What we have conventionally referred to as "popular" culture can be seen as a field on which such negotiations of cultural significance have been conducted. More to the point, I am in agreement with those who see *television* as the central symbol field in contemporary American culture. Many of our shared meanings, our basic values, are "discussed" and "debated" there in the contexts of entertainment and information.

IN DEFENSE OF "POPULAR"

Now let me digress for a moment to point out some of the implications of this notion. Almost anyone who thinks about it for a moment will agree that the content of television, as the content of popular culture generally throughout our history, is made up of mixtures of current problems, old ideas, familiar forms, novel expressions and so on. The tendency, however, has been to consider these presentations as inferior, as simplistic, crude, or as the expressions of dominant forces in a conservative culture. Pick your epithet. Such perjorative distinctions extend, whether we intend them to or not, to the people involved with the popular culture materials, the mass audience. We suggest in various subtle and not-so-subtle ways that "they" do not "appreciate" the appropriate objects, by which we may mean those that often please "us." We suggest that they are seduced by the simplicity, the tawdry baubles, bright beads and blankets, foisted on them by unscrupulous traders hungry for profit and power. Most often this is not an intentional discrimination, but the view is a strong part of our cultural heritage.

The symbols I have used to describe this attitude should call us up short. The analogy is clearly to our ethnocentric view of other peoples, to our exploitation of cultures and nations in the name of a presumed moral, political, financial, or ethical superiority. I do not wish to be mistaken on this point. The discriminatory view that I have described is a prevalent one *within* the entertainment industry, and great evils are justified in the name of "giving the audience what it wants." But the view is equally powerful in the rhetoric of educators, reform groups, and interest groups that must be accurately defined as working in their own rather than the public interest.

What we should see, given the history of gross social errors in other areas, is that "popular," rather than indicating inferior product or audience, must indicate different. Levi-Strauss has made us aware that what we have referred to as the "savage mind," is actually a powerful complexity, a logic, a history, a way of understanding and shaping the world. I am willing to argue that there is an equally powerful complexity in popular culture generally, in television specifically. This complexity is directly related to the cultural, the public nature of popular materials. It is one of the ways in which we continually re-think our world, re-create it in the public sphere so that it can be shared. The distinction is elegantly outlined by Carey writing:

> In our predominantly individualistic tradition, we are accustomed to think of thought as essentially private, an activity that occurs in the head—graphically represented by Rodin's "The Thinker." I wish to suggest, in contradistinction, that thought is predominantly public and social. It occurs primarily on blackboards, in dances, and recited poems. The capacity of private thought is a derived, and secondary talent, one that appears biographically later in the person and historically later in the species. Thought is public because it depends on a publicly available stock of symbols. (1, p. 15).

To Carey's blackboards, dances, and recited poems, we must now add television in all its forms. It is our most publicly available stock of symbols.

UNDERSTANDING TELEVISION

This brings us to a crucial point in examining television as popular culture. Our public symbol system, viewed as a whole, is as complex, confused, contradictory as are our other systems. Symbols have multiple meanings, even in what appear to be the most simple combinations. Dealing with them in the private nature of our individual thoughts or in the public arena of the classroom means that we have to untangle those complexities. Let me illustrate this with some examples from television. Some are merely telling anecdotes, others are more thorough analysis.

Some time ago I attended a meeting that brought together a combination of interested citizens, professional educators, some of whom were television scholars, and industry representatives including independent television producers. One of my friends found himself seated for lunch with some representatives from a local PTA group who discussed their television monitoring programs and their own views of television. The discussion turned to specific shows. One of the programs angrily criticized was *The Rockford Files*. Now my friend is especially fond of the incredible range of detective shows on television and in its history, finding it the form most suited to television's particular aesthetic demands. He asked if their negative view could explain the deep and loving relationship between Rockford and his father, which is an essential aspect of the show's formula. They were not able to respond to his satisfaction because they were intent on isolating and discussing only one aspect of the program. Indeed, they indicated that such a question had never occurred to them and might be somewhat absurd. The story is made much more interesting, I think, by the fact that an NBC Vice-President was also seated at the table and it was clear that such a question had never occurred to him either. He was visibly amused at my friend's passion for the show and his insistence that it is a complex symbol system drawing on tradition, emotion and current attitudes. I tell the story to raise the question of how the loving relationship between father and son, presented to a society that needs stronger images of such male relationships, can modify our understanding of the images of the sometimes violent white male authority figure, an image that is needed less in the same society.

In a similar vein we could analyze the much maligned *Starsky* and *hutch*. Most reaction to this program also focuses on excessive violence. Little of it examines the depth of mutual support between the central characters. They are, literally, quite willing to die for one another, and in the name of the affection are willing to violate authority, norm, and legal guideline. Is this good or bad? Does it modify the use of violence, shade it in significant ways? Does it elevate the worth of individuals and the sanctity of human commitment over the rules of social order that sometimes ignore individual value? Why are the characters never allowed to develop equally complex relationships with other individuals, especially females? Is this, as some analysts have suggested, a "muted homoeroticism?" Or is it a continuation of that very old pattern in American culture, the pattern of male support in stressful, especially violent situations? The questions do not arise, I hasten to add, only from popular entertainment forms. They would not appear there if they did not plague us in day-to-day life, in the making of policy about financial support for female athletic programs, about the role of toys and school curricula in the shaping of sex role expectations, about the authority of males in religious institutions, about the worth of all individuals and the sacrifices demanded of us in protecting that worth.

Similar complexities arise from a program such as *Kojak*. Let me narrate for you one of my favorite episodes and examine it somewhat more closely than I have these other examples. Bad heroin has hit the streets of the city. Several addicts die, among them some prostitutes. Kojak asks special permission to pursue the case more intently and the permission is denied. He is outraged because he senses the real motivation behind the denial; no one cares if a few more junkies and hookers die. Soon, however, two white, teenaged girls die in a posh suburban home after shooting up with the same drug. Now the authorities have their turn at outrage. Kojak is commissioned to break the case with all possible speed.

There is a sub-plot. Kojak has been offered a job as chief of security of a major insurance firm. The job carries wealth and prestige, assistance of every sort, all the luxuries a law enforcement professional could desire. He is sorely tempted. The streets are wearing him down and the official police system, in decisions such as the one related, is no better.

The two stories come together when we learn that one of the sons of the insurance company's executive family is involved in the importation of the bad dope. He is not a professional pusher. For him it is a lark, mere excitement. Kojak, of course, cracks the case and will not bargain with the wealthy family. He refuses the inducement of the job which is offered in exchange for altering the charges. In the end we see him leaving the gleaming glass tower where the corrupt power brokers still reside and moving back to his real home, the streets of the city. At one point in the episode Kojak explains his feelings, his sense that the prostitutes and junkies are as important as suburban teenagers, by saying, "All God's children, Baby, all God's children."

What are we to do with *this* conglomeration of symbols? We have explicit religious references throughout the show. They are not all even as thinly veiled as the implication of Theo Kojak's name. Most of them are blatant surface indicators. We have a direct claim in the plot that outsiders—criminals—may be seen as victims of social process as well. We have the argument that the social status of individuals should in no way diminish the significance of their human worth. We have an overt attack on an economic elite depicted as self-interested, manipulative, exploitative, frivolous in the most vicious sense. And many of these condemnations, charges, and attacks come from the mouth, as usual, of a powerful white male figure who bulls his way through the world with what can only be termed gaudy condescension. One could lecture on the entire history of American culture using such a program as the central text, for its story is as old as America itself.

But why should any of this be surprising. In hindsight we know that other stories of crime and detection of adventure and romance, have been a central locus of cultural commentary. The question is not how such presentations tell the truth, but rather, how they comment on issues in our collective life. And the same questions can be raised by all the other popular cultural forms.

When an old man dies in Archie Bunker's living room and jokes are made for a few moments we sense a kind of disease that moves us toward larger issues. But then Archie walks onto his front porch, wraps his arms about his body, looks off into the night, and says to Edith, "I'm cold." I know that it is not the cold of an autumn night in Queens that he refers to. It is the coldness that grips all of us when we wake suddenly to the realization of our terminal case of life. It is presented in such a way that the meaning is evident for all audiences.

Or consider another layering of complexities. Much of the discussion of the *Mary Tyler Moore Show* has had to do with whether or not we have there the depiction of truly changing attitudes toward women or merely a more subtle maintenance of the present system of discrimination. That topic is crucial to the show and can be worked out. I do not think, however, that it can be worked out unless we realize that the show is as much about families as it is about women. What we see there is the extension of family values of love, support, sacrifice, and honor to a non-biological group, a work force, the market place of labor. That which was once reserved for blood ties is now seen to order other relations as well. Perhaps it is in this way that we will negotiate new terms through which to understand men and women better, by realizing that we are indeed linked by larger familial ties. What such presentations indicate is that we are seeing these issues in process, in moments of change and dispute.

With this in mind I would like to close this series of examples by attending to a different arena. This one, I think, demonstrates even more graphically than others what I mean by our use of television as a ground for public thinking. For this example is an unself-conscious kind of presentation rather than one designed to call up the ideas we've looked at. At a recent conference on Television and the Family an NBC Vice President indicated, almost in passing, that one subject drawing heavy negative mail commentary is the advertisement of what the industry euphemistically refers to as "feminine protection items." This category includes all items associated with menstruation. Most of the people discussing this subject with him found such criticism narrow or short sighted. Yet in a discussion group later that day one woman expressed clear sympathy with the negative responses to such ads. She referred to the embarrassment experienced by her fourteen year old daughter when such advertisements appeared during family group viewing. Another woman immediately responded by suggesting that the embarrassment was exactly the problem. Her view was that no woman, girl, man or boy *should* be embarrassed in such a situation. While criticizing the ads for their particular form, she praised them for bringing to the surface an issue too long considered taboo. My own point is that the response to television's role in the matter of this small example must be fully related to the larger cultural issue, to incredibly old and complex questions involving the entire history of male-female relations, and more importantly, to current changes in those relations. In so relatively minor a fashion as this, television is central to that process and is neither cause, effect, nor answer to the problems that arise.

It is this failure to recognize the cultural context of television that rises at every stage of every discussion of the medium. This failure is at the heart of Benjamin Stein's incredibly flawed book, *The View From Sunset Boulevard* (3). Stein appears to know nothing of American history and culture. He certainly exhibits no knowledge that the conflicts he toys with are deep rooted American conflicts that have never been settled.

And the creators of television hardly do better. In extended conversations with producers, the creative controllers of television, and with representatives of internal network censor offices, I have found varying degrees of awareness regarding the cultural contextualization of the medium. Most producers intentionally include moral, ethical, and political messages in their programs. The ideas are most often reflections of their individual values. Generally, however, they are unaware of other factors that affect those messages. They are unaware that the use of certain formulas, certain types of heroes, certain images, may work precisely in the opposite direction of their intentions. Only in the case of the most self-conscious producers are all these factors taken into account.

THE TRANSACTION OF COMMUNICATION

Even when they are, however, there is no ultimate control of the meaning and use of those ideas, those clusters of symbols and values. For we have dealt to this point only with the process of production and transmission of meanings. At the other end of the process is the audience, and the complexities are as profound here as in the origination of content. No matter how skillful the producer or programmer of television in their attempts to universalize their audiences, there is no ultimate control over how those products are received, decoded, shared and internalized.

Individuals decode messages and each does so within a maze of overlapping relationships. We can refer to this process as "making sense," and our emphasis should be on the fact that individuals do make, create, meanings of their own. They are developing structures of values and beliefs that allow them to live in groups, to be members of society, and yet maintain a private sense of self. Groups, whether they are families, school fellows, church organizations, office staffs, crews, or teams, will somehow have some influence on the interpretation and use of the symbols received by individuals. Similarly, differing levels of education, differing degrees of historical knowledge and critical abilities play a role. Every factor becomes another variable in what the receiver does with content. I do not want to overemphasize this point. We do not live in a chaotic welter of individual worlds. There are ranges of meaning that circumscribe what we see and allow us to communicate. Indeed, this is what the producer aims at, the widest possible *shared* meaning, and this is what accounts for the familiarity, the repetition, the copying in popular culture discourse. There are always dominant meanings preferred by those who hold power over communication. But there is no assurance that those are the meanings that get to the audience. As a result of this process we should look for *meanings in action*. It is at the juncture of choice, where potentially contradictory messages must be translated into activity, that culture is made, that true effects appear. And it is at this point that my second major term, criticism, plays its crucial role.

REACTIONARY EDUCATION

The alternative to a critically based program of television studies is what I call reactionary education. We react to television and build a curriculum out of that reaction. In this model television is the enemy and children are educated in self defense. If we study a subject, we process it, identify our appreciation and enjoyment, rid ourselves of guilt induced by unwarranted social assumptions, understand our negative responses, take the subject into our minds as something that we can, as humans who think critically, control.

The reactionary view portends little in the way of true skills. Indeed, such a view is hardly education at all in any deep sense. Let me rely on an analogy I have found useful. In an earlier call for a massive program of television education I suggested that American society has experienced two spectacular failures in facing commonly defined social problems. Television is one, sex is the other. Now if we follow the reactionary model we can imagine an adequate sex education program, but I think that none of us would consider mere propholaxis to be true sex education. Military sex films accomplish a task, but hardly in a way that encourages rich, complex, rewarding knowledge of sexuality in one's life.

TELEVISION AND CRITICAL THINKING

Please do not misunderstand. I do not think or mean to imply that anyone at our conference has or will support such crude models of television education. Rather I am suggesting that television education, like all the best education, must transcend its subject. This suggestion is contrary to a popular attitude in which calls for television education are considered silly. From this perspective, television is patently simple and anyone who has received a good general education should be able to do the sort of minimal analysis necessary in order to protect himself. I think this view is an impoverished one. It ignores the influence that a critically aware audience can have on the function of the medium in society. It slights the subject matter. It is rooted in condescension.

Yet there is a truth to the comment. Critical thinking as a way of living in the world is not subject matter specific. It can be taught on any base, at all levels. Most often it has been taught as we are taught to write clearly and effectively. As teachers have abdicated that responsibility critical powers may have diminished. (Note that television rather than responsible human beings has often been blamed for the decline, as if the ability to write were innate and could be drained away.) The opportunity open to us now is to use the television education curricula to once again place critical thinking at the center of our educational programs. In doing so we should remember that critical skills are the true base for a true sense of working in the public interest, even when they lead students to disagree with us.

There are multiple ironies here. The most apparent is that the instrument often blamed for a decline in reading, writing, and critical thinking can easily be used to renew those skills in more powerful ways. There is *no* television program that does not lend itself to close, extended analysis.

But the more profound irony is that if we choose reaction over criticism we will be guilty of exactly the same defect we attribute to television. We will be indoctrinating our children. They might grow up to turn off the TV set. But we will have done little to enable them to avoid our own errors when the next new technology, with all its attendant problems, bulges into their lives.

To ignore the complexities found in television as a part of culture, to avoid the hard task of teaching critical skills, is to condemn students to simplistic responses in a complex world. As a scholar—critic of television and popular culture I find that intellectually fraudulent. As a teacher I find it lazy. As a parent I find it morally myopic. And as a citizen I can support nothing less than a full critically based curriculum of television studies for our schools.

REFERENCES

1. Carey, J. A cultural approach to communication. *communication*, 1975, 2, 1-22.
2. Eisenstein, E. *Printing press as an agent of change.* New York: Cambridge University Press, 1979.
3. Stein, B. *The view from Sunset Boulevard.* New York: Basic Books, 1979.

Receivership Skills: An Educational Response

James A. Anderson

INTRODUCTION

Modern theoretical perspectives on the mass media have moved away from the concept of the all-powerful media holding in their hypnotic glow the lives of each and every one of us. Television, newspapers, magazines and the cinema are surely part of our lives as are indoor plumbing, the automobile and inflation. Each affects the way we think, value things, and behave. But each of these influences is managed by the individual for the purpose that he or she chooses. Consider these three actual scenes we have observed in our program of television research:

Scene One

"Hey, I'm home" The slam of the door left no doubt that indeed Melissa was home from another day of being a third grader "What's to eat; I'm starving?" "Your snack is on the table, Lis." Melissa crossed to the kitchen, turned on the small TV set and sat down to eat. A game show was in progress which she watched with little reaction. Her mother came into the kitchen and busied herself with some ever-present task. Melissa did little to acknowledge her presence. Some twenty minutes after she arrived home,

---

James A. Anderson, Ph.D. is Professor of Communication and Direction of the Division of Journalism and Mass Communication at the University of Utah. He was a co-director of the conference.

Melissa pushed the plate away, turned off the TV and walked over to her mother and gave her a hug. "That was good, Mom." "Well, I'm glad you liked it. How was your day at school?" "It was OK. We did the neatest thing in reading today. It was about TV commercials."

Melissa was part of a group of children who had kept a diary of their television viewing over a two-week period. When she shared her diary with us, we were intrigued by the regular pattern of the set going on at about 3:15 and off before 4:00. As we talked with her, the pattern of behavior, described in scenario above, emerged. We asked her what she watched. "Whatever is on," she replied. We asked her why she watched TV. "To keep me company while I eat." We talked to her mother who told us that such was the usual ritual when Melissa came home, and that by waiting for her to finish her snack before talking to her, she found Melissa much more interested in conversing about her day.

Scene Two

Each weekday afternoon at 5:00 the doorbell rang followed immediately by an impatient knock. "That's got to be Eric; right on time," she said as she got up to answer the door. "Come on in; Amy and Eden are already downstairs with Angela." Eric, the four-year-old, next-door-neighbor, was dressed, as always, with an apron around his shoulders for a cape, vinyl cowboy boots and his gun belt wrapped twice around his shorts. He was dressed as his favorite superhero; it was time to watch the show.

Eric joined the three children downstairs. After watching for a few minutes they began to act out part of the scene they were watching. The television became a backdrop for their own play activity. When a particularly exciting scene came on, they would stop to watch and then go back to play. The television show was over long before the playing stopped.

Scene Three

John Roberts quickly flipped the bicycle over and stood it on the seat and handle bars. He was hurrying now because it was already after 10:00. He loosened the bolts on the back wheel and pulled it off the bike. He grabbed the tube repair kit and the pump and hurried into the house. "We'll be ready with half-time highlights of yesterday's games in just one minute," the television set announced. "Just made it," he thought.

Roberts felt pretty pleased with himself. Since dinner he had gotten part of the garage cleaned and was now ready to fix his young son's tire—all in time for the favorite part of the weekly nighttime football game. As the highlights came on, he watched intently. There had been quite a bit of talk at work about one of the Sunday games. He wanted to see the disputed call as it was sure to engender more discussion. The highlights over, the second half started. Roberts worked on the tire during the commercial breaks and when there was little action on the field. The instant replay made sure he'd have plenty of chance to see any excitement.

FUNDAMENTAL PROPOSITIONS OF RECEIVERSHIP SKILLS CURRICULA

These three scenes exemplify three very different uses of television, conditions of viewing, and sources of satisfaction. Televiewing has long passed the novelty stage and is now woven into the fabric of most Americans' daily lives. Television has been successful, as all mass media, because it can serve a large number of different purposes. It is neither specialized nor demanding. If we could, with an omniscient author's eye, peer into the homes of some 60 million viewers we would find nearly that many reasons for viewing. Here is a woman filling time waiting for her husband to finish getting ready to go out. Here is another deeply engrossed in some continuing drama. Here is a worker letting himself relax before bed. Here are two children pretending to be involved in a program to avoid going to bed. All of our viewers may be watching the same program. Each comes to view with a particular set of motivations and receptivity. The consequences of viewing will vary directly with those differing motivational and receptivity states. The understandings that they gain and the satisfactions they draw from viewing may be substantially different. The key to understanding the relation between what is presented and what results is that *content is a poor predictor of effect.*

The notion that the same content can produce different effects in different people is older than the biblical parable of the sower of seeds. The fact that our research literature is full of contradictory findings can easily lead one to conclude that there are no strong consistent effects of viewing television which can be systematically associated with large segments of the viewing audience. Rather there appear to be particular effects which are associated with given motivational, attitudinal and cognitive states of the receiver. And as those states change from time to time or even moment to moment the consequences of interpretation of televised messages change.

Each child's viewing then is highly individualistic. Consider the following scenario drawn from a lesson presented on *Sesame Street* (2). This lesson was apparently designed to point out how important friends are to one's happiness. The principal characters in the segment were the puppets Bert and Ernie and the real-life person Maureen. The segment begins with Bert and Ernie arguing about the rights to a cookie that is in Ernie's possession. To prevent Bert from getting any, Ernie quickly eats the cookie; whereupon Bert informs Ernie that he will never speak to him again and pokes Ernie in the stomach. Because of the disagreement, they decide to terminate their friendship and pursue lives as far apart from each other as possible—one chooses the North Pole; the other will become a cowboy. Maureen enters and points out how empty and lonely their lives will be without one another. Bert feels guilty and apologizes to Ernie for his aggressive behavior. Ernie reminds Bert that he was positive that the cookie was his. Bert asks Ernie how he can be so sure, to which Ernie counters, "Because I ate yours this morning."

The nature of this scene can generate a large number of interpretations and consequent effects. One child may key in on how clever Ernie is. Not only did he get both cookies but he also got away with it with little more than an argument. This child's own experience with friends or siblings might reinforce that view and consequently the lesson will simply help maintain that behavior.

Another child might focus on the lesson that Bert might have learned. This child may perceive that people seldom really care about one another and consequently may find the final exchange where Ernie admits having eaten Bert's cookie earlier in the day to be entirely consistent with behavior or incidents he has observed.

Finally, a third child may perceive the segment exactly as intended—that people indeed are more important than possessions and that one should not be willing to abandon a friendship because of a dispute over a material object, however important at the moment. Because of the child's situational and psychological condition at the time, the content may even be perceived to have a great deal of application to her own behavior.

These explanations demonstrate that content may be pro-social in intent and nature but the applications by the viewers may not. The interpretations and consequences of viewing depend as much or more on the circumstances of the viewer than on the content of the program.

As we begin this consideration of the role of education and television we need to state a fundamental proposition: People do things *with* television; television does not do things *to* people. People choose to use television and the influences of television can be managed. The business of education is to provide the skills to choose wisely and manage well. We are charged with the consideration of the skills which are useful in the management of communication messages which inform, entertain, persuade. Television is our focus today, but the issues transcend the medium of presentation. The skills we teach must be relevant to the entire system of communication in which our society operates. Such is the notion of receivership skills.

RECEIVERSHIP SKILLS DEFINED

Receivership skills refers to those skills related to the assimilation and utilization of communication messages for some purposeful action. They involve the skillful collection, interpretation, testing and application of information regardless of medium of presentation. Skills of this nature have had an extensive educational history. Current educational thought treats them under the rubrics of critical reading and critical thinking.

Receivership skills enlarge both of these notions by conceptualizing the individual as a consumer of information. As a knowledgeable consumer the individual has need of common skills of analysis (as in critical thinking) medium specific skills of reception and interpretation (as in critical reading for print materials) and content specific skills of understanding.

We live in a complex communication system. Information comes to the individual in a variety of packages. That combination is different from the sum of the parts, creating a unique communication event to which the individual responds. An election campaign, for example, may find an individual responding to televised, printed and interpersonal messages which may be complimenatry or contradictory, suggesting different actions grounded in different motives. Focusing on a single medium as we will during the next few days is clearly useful to advance that area, but it is also clearly inadequate for understanding the individual operating in a technologically advanced system. Hence our consideration of the larger construct of receivership skills.

Perhaps it would be useful to begin a description of those skills as applied to television by contrasting them with what they are not. They are not rules of when to view, what to view, or how long to view. They are not the imposition of elitist notions of intrinsic values residing in a medium of presentation such as print or in specific content types. They are not the generation of anxiety or guilt over the uses one has for the medium and its content.

Receivership skills begin with those skills needed to identify and understand our own motives and purposes for attendance. They include the ability to interpret the influence of those motives and purposes on the way we make sense of the messages we receive. That those motives, for example, may facilitate the acceptance of certain statements and the rejection of others.

They provide the ability to grasp the meaning of the message; to comprehend language and visual and aural images discriminately; to interpret "hidden" meanings; to specify the working elements of the message; to identify to whom the message is directed and its intent.

They foster the observation of details their sequence and relationships; the understanding of themes, values, motivating elements, plotlines, characters and characterization.

They direct the evaluation of fact, opinion, logical and affective appeals. They identify fanciful writing and images.

Receivership skills include an understanding of the sources of bias inherent in the medium of presentation, and a comprehension of the grammar, syntax and meanings contained in the methods chosen to produce the message.

Finally, the individual trained in receivership skills can recognize intended affective reactions and motives; can relegate personal value to the message; identify emotional satisfactions and their sources in the messages; relate the message to other experiences and information; can make inferences, draw conclusions and establish predictions or other criteria for evaluation.

When we view the teaching of receivership skills as an educational response to the tensions induced by television and other media, we rest on two assumptions: (1) that children can utilize certain viewing skills and analytical procedures to modify source, message and medium effects toward pro-social consequences and (2) that these skills and procedures can be taught in the ordinary classroom using curricular materials and instructional approaches specially designed for that purpose.

PROJECTED OUTCOMES

The critical viewing projects that are in progress now and report later in this volume represent a major test of the notion that the effect of a communication can be controlled by modifying the assimilation and analytical skills of the receiver. The success of this test has important implications for the social control of information, the structure of communication systems, their potential role in the socialization of the child, the development of consumer skills and the impact on political and economic systems of an informed citizenry. For a moment, let us consider what those implications might be.

Social Control of Information

For most the social control of information is a nettlesome issue. On the one hand there is concern over the manipulation possible by sophisticated communicators of naive audiences as in the potential case of advertising to children. On the other, there is the realization of the clear and present danger of censoring review boards. The United States has consistently reached for the ideal of the free market place of ideas whether political, religious or commercial. But the concept of the free market place requires that both the buyer and the seller be on equal footing lest there be exploitation. Protection of the free flow of information is enhanced when the conditions of possible exploitation and the consequent need for censorship are reduced. A skillful audience is, of course, less open to exploitation.

Communication Systems

The present structure of our communication system is the consequence of the interplay of forces of technology, government regulation, economics, management and the audience. Of all of these the audience has been least understood and the least organized in producing a coherent influence. Yet the audience is the most socially significant and that which the others supposedly serve. Widespread adoption of critical receivership skills curricula holds the portent of a knowledgeable and knowable audience shaping the content and delivery systems of a communications revolution already begun.

Socialization

Socialization is the primary activity of family, peer groups and social institutions. Compared with the normal workings of these influence the influence of television can be compared to turning on a flashlight on a bright sunny day. It certainly adds light to the scene but its effect is trivial. Should the child, however, be removed from the normal circumstances of family, friends and school he moves into the shadows and that flashlight can become a beacon. Children as they pass through the socialization process can find themselves in periods of intense change where the need for information exceeds the capacity of the interpersonal environment to provide it or the individual may find herself with reduced contact with that environment. Our observational studies provide a good example (4). These studies involve working with families as they watch television. In one family, with a history of one job transfer after another, the 12 year old daughter's favorite programs were those which had main characters of her age. The daughter noted that she liked those programs because they helped her learn what to do in different situations. While the young woman was in no way handicapped socially, her friendships tended to be less secure and, consequently, less useful for social learning. The television program became her laboratory providing ideas and the means for testing them.

Even without special circumstances younger children are continually striving for information about the world of older children that they are about to enter. My younger daughter was explaining to me what it means to "park." She said, "First you turn the radio on loud. Then you find some place dark and open the windows. Then you get close together and kiss, I guess." When asked how she knew all this, she replied, "Oh, I learned it all on *Happy Days*." Her story crystallized for me the preconditions for social learning: First, there has to be an interest or need on the part of the child. Second the program content has to be appropriate to the child's information requirements and to the child's ability to understand. And, third if the information is going to stand the test of utility the author must have creatively captured the essence of the event or interaction.

Clearly this process is open to modification by providing content and analytical skills. We can better prepare our children to select and test social information.

Consumer Socialization

A genuine concern of teachers and parents alike is that young children do not distinguish between program content and commercial content. American commercial television receives its income based on the size of the audience delivered into the hands of national advertisers who respond with a message in which every element has been selected for its capacity to sell. It is, of course, the "intent to sell" which is the primary distinguishing characteristic of the commercial. It is a characteristic which children can readily learn.

It is not necessary to take the position that children are ignorant lambs in the marketplace. Children typically show themselves to be capable of making market decisions to select products which meet their demands.

Their criteria may not always agree with ours, but their criteria are usually justified.

I observed one five-year old boy sing along with a gum commercial. After it was over I asked him if he would like some of that gum. "Nah," he replied, "I tried that once and it was icky."

Clearly, however there are circumstances in which a child's limited experience may lead him to be more susceptible to the blandishments of commercial advertising. Children under nine do not necessarily understand the product implications of the phrases: "Some assembly required." "Items sold separately." "Batteries not included." Changes in image size can be interpreted as changes in actual size so that a candy bar in close-up may be perceived as larger (1). Spokespersons may be seen as objective commentators.

We as teachers and parents can provide the solution for these problems. The commercial is a limited (albeit important) information source from a particular point of view. It is intended to sell the viewer; it is susceptible to deceptive practices; it is not required to tell "the whole story." It will emphasize the good and not report the bad; it is not responsible to the consumer but to the seller; it is often times attractive, subtle and deals in compelling motivations; and as an information source it has little competition. These facts form a primer for the competent viewer and consumer. The development of their understanding is certainly a consequence for the student of receivership skills.

Citizens and the Media

Our final consideration is the provision for an informed citizenry. News is a commodity, bought, sold and delivered. As with any commodity its quality is set by the demands of the consumers. For children, news of import pertains to school, family and friends. Few children have great need for national and international news. The young and older adult clearly does. Training in receivership skills cannot stop in our grade schools. It is exceedingly important that for the individual who must use the news to make decisions to understand the limitations of each information source and to pursue a comparative analysis in the development of knowledge and opinion. The technology and practices of the news industry continue to change, affecting the structure, biases and limitations of the information presented. The skillful analysis of information is a life-long learning requirement of an informed citizenry functioning in an economic and political system where individual choice is the currency of note.

The teaching of critical receivership skills is a contribution our school systems can make to the good progress of society. Television, radio, newspapers, magazines, and the cinema are significant elements in our lives. We need to be sophisticated about their biases and their insights.

References

1. Acker, S. Tiemens, R. Conservation of televised images: A developmental study. Paper presented to the Society of Research and Child Development, San Francisco, 1979.

2. Anderson, J.A., Meyer, T., and Donohue, T.R. The wheel comes to social science: A model relating mass communication research to social policy planning. *Communication* (in press).

3. Anderson, J.A. and Ploghoft, M.E. *The way we see it*. Athens, Ohio: Social Science Cooperative Center, 1978.

4. Anderson, J.A., Traudt, P., Acker, S., Meyer, T., and Donohue, T.R. An ethnological approach to a study of televiewing in family settings. Paper presented to the Western Speech Communication Association, Los Angeles, 1979.

The Child as Viewer

Ellen Wartella

INTRODUCTION

The truthfulness of the statement that children think differently than adults is fairly self evident. Any adult who has spent even passing time with a preschooler or elementary school child recognizes that young children are not miniature adults. Moreover, not all children are alike—during the course of childhood, children change radically in the ways they perceive and interact with the world around them. A four-year old is different from a six-year old who is different from a ten-and fourteen-year old. The more limited cognitive abilities and more limited social experiences of the four-year old makes him/her quite different viewers of television from a ten year old or adult. Thus, anyone who discusses the "child" as viewer must first ask the question which child are you asking about, the young preschooler, the early elementary-schooler, the child at which age level? The major focus of this discussion, then, is the nature of the development of children as viewers of television.

Ellen Wartella, Ph.D. is Research Assistant Professor, Institute of Communications Research, University of Illinois at Urbana-Champaign.

TELEVISION AND DEVELOPMENT

The goal of this presentation is to sketch, albeit very briefly, some of the dimensions of age-related changes in how child viewers interact with television. During the course of childhood, children are undergoing vast changes in the ways in which they think about and interact with their world. The growth of thinking abilities, the increasing history, social experiences and other social and affective changes are reflected in the ways in which children of different ages both use and understand television messages. My interest then is *not* to talk about what television does to children, but rather to talk about what children of different ages as viewers of television *do with* television.

Specifically, then I am focusing on how children's developing cognitive abilities and social experiences lead to increasingly better understanding of television programs, of television characters and of the differing kinds of television content. I have chosen to try to do this by describing and comparing three major age groups of child viewers: the preschooler or child under age five; the early, elementary school child viewer, or children between ages five and eight; and the late elementary school child viewer, those between ages nine and twelve. My grouping of child viewers into these three age ranges may seem somewhat arbritary, but I do think that they are representative of major epochs in the development of various sorts of understanding of the medium of television.

Although there have been various studies of children's use of television (15), examination of age-related changes in children's understanding of television messages is a relatively recent topic for research. Furthermore, most of this research has occurred within the last ten years. Therefore, many gaps in our ability to identify precisely age-related changes in how children make sense of television will be found. However, with this caveat in mind, let me attempt to describe what I think we do know regarding how children between preschool and late elementary school interact with television: how they use the medium and how they understand the medium.

The Preschool as Viewer

Children are very early introduced to television most likely by their parents who prop them in front of the TV set as toddlers. There is evidence (1,5,8,9,12) that approximately 14 per cent of two-year old American children regularly attend to television. By age four, this precentage has increased to about two-thirds. Television very early becomes the predominant medium used by very young children.

Most recent estimates (5) of the amount of time preschoolers spend with television suggests that between ages two and five, children spend more time with television (approximately 29 hours per week according to Nielsen figures) than do older children between six and eleven (26.7 hours per week). Television viewing for preschoolers averages about three and three quarter hours per day.

Several observational studies of children's attention to television indicate that it is as early as these preschool years that children begin to develop adult-like TV "watching" patterns. Anderson et al., (2) notes that up until about age two-and-one-half children tend to orient themselves away from the television set with few looks at the screen. Starting at about two-and-one-half, however, children begin to orient themselves toward the TV screen, and begin to monitor the set frequently. Preschool children generally tend to look at the set for short periods, less than three seconds, and their attention is variable. Factors which affect their looking or not looking include the presence of other distractions in the room, such as toys, the content of the television (in particular audio changes tend to increase attention), and the comprehensibility of the message. The evidence indicates that children as young as ages two and three attended less to segments of a *Sesame Street* program that were rendered less intelligible than to more comprehensible segments of the program.

But what of the preschoolers understanding of the television messages they are watching? There is considerable evidence to indicate that preschool children are severely limited in the ways in which they construe meanings of television content.

Perhaps the major limitation on the young preschoolers interpretations of television messages, is their difficulty in distinguishing the reality and fantasy of television portrayals. In particular, evidence indicates that preschoolers have difficulty distinguishing television people as actors, and not as real people with whom to interact in play and real life. TV to children in this age group is a "magic window on the world" (7).

Preschoolers interpretations of dramatic plotlines and program messages are probably fairly idiosyncratic: they have difficulty interpreting and understanding narratives, scene development and character motivations for behavior (4).

Moreover, it appears (1) that preschoolers have very rudimentary understanding of the various kinds of programming on television. They may have difficulty distinguishing programs from commercials, for instance, and primarily do so with reference to the visual, surface characteristics of the two kinds of content.

In short, the young, preschool child viewer of television is severely limited, at least relative to older children and adults, in the way they construe meaning from television. Nevertheless, it is during the preschool years that children become regular viewers of the medium.

The Early Elementary Schooler: Ages Five Through Eight

Between ages five and eight, or roughly kindergarten and third grade, children undergo substantial changes in their understanding of television. Furthermore, it is during these years that children's TV content preferences are changing. What kinds of shows are children interested in at these age levels? Studies (5) indicate that cartoons, situation comedies and family situation shows account for over 70 per cent of first graders program preferences. Children's tastes in programs during this epoch are very much associated with comedy and humor. And, these children are now beginning to move away from children's shows toward more prime-time viewing (16).

Children between five and eight are acquiring new levels of understanding of television. For instance, Hawkins (7) reports that between first and third grades children realize that television is not a "magic window" on the world, as the preschooler and kindergarteners are reported to discuss television's reality. Yet there is evidence that children in this age range still perceive television people and events as being like real life—that is, while they may be actors, they act like real people.

Children between kindergarten and third grade still show difficulties in understanding the content of television. Evidence (3) indicates that children during these years have difficulty indentifying and remembering information adults consider essential to understanding dramatic plotlines and that they may be making little attempt to organize plotline information to try to make sense of dramatic narratives. The more complex social cues, character motivations for actions and social situations portrayed on television may be interpreted by children in this age range in relatively limited ways, perhaps with reference to stereotypical expectations about television people (4).

Two other areas in which five to eight-year old children's understanding of television is limited compared to older children is in their ability to articulate distinctions among various kinds of television production techniques and programming contents. For instance, it is quite likely that even children as old as seven or eight still have very rudimentary understanding of the various audio-visual techniques employed in television productions, such as zooms, pans, slow motion and other audiovisual symbols (6,11,13,17).

Furthermore, although it is between the ages of five and eight years that the majority of children can begin to articulate the notion that advertising content is different from other programming on television because advertising sells products, it is yet unlikely that children in this age range take the advertiser's point of view into account when viewing an advertisement (10).

Thus, between ages five and eight children begin to prefer more adult oriented television programs. They are still rather limited in their perceptions and interpretations of the television messages. These limitations may lead to a different understanding of television by the early elementary school child viewer.

The Late-Elementary Schooler: Ages Nine Through Twelve
It is during the later elementary school years that children's viewing and understanding of television messages more clearly approximate adult-like patterns—although children in this age range still evidence some particular

difficulties in coping with the television medium.

For instance, although children continue to enjoy comedies through adolescence and adulthood, by sixth grade, dramatic shows are popular sorts of television fare (5). Similarly, while the audience for any Saturday morning show may be primarily children under twelve, in actuality children in this age range watch prime time television more than Saturday morning programming (5).

Similarly, children between ages nine and twelve are developing more complete and differentiated understanding of television messages and television characters. Between third and sixth grades children begin to examine television characters' motivations for actions (16). Compared to preschooler and younger elementary school aged children, these older children, are better able to order scenes of plot lines, to recognize and select scenes adults consider essential to understanding the narrative and are more likely to evaluate characters' behavior in terms of the consequences and the motivations for the behaviors. By fifth grade, children appear to be organizing and trying to make sense of plot line information (3).

In summary, during the late-elementary school years child viewers are increasingly more sophisticated in their interpretations of television and television messages. The medium, however, is not completely well understood. For instance, even by sixth grade understanding of the basic economic relationship among television programming, advertising and viewership (6,14), or the business of television is still somewhat limited. Certainly, however, these relatively older children would appear to be more competent viewers of television than younger child viewers.

CONCLUSION

This brief review of the various sorts of age-related changes in children's use of and interpretations of television should indicate something of the wide range of competencies for dealing with television messages demonstrated by child viewers. The child viewer of television is not easily described as a single type of viewer, rather between the early preschool years, and later, elementary school years, children have much to learn in developing their use and understanding of the medium of television.

References

1. Adler, R.P., *et al.* Research on the effects of television advertising on children: A review of the literature and recommendations for future research. Washington, D.C.: National Science Foundation, 1977.

2. Anderson, D.R., *et al.* Watching children watch television. In G. Hale and M. Lewis (eds.) *Attention and the development of cognitive skills.* New York: Poenum publishing, 1979.

3. Collins, W.A. Children's comprehension of television content. In E. Wartella (ed.) *Children communication: Media and development of thought, speech and understanding.* Beverly Hills: Sage, 1979.

4. Collins, W.A. Social knowledge and processing of social information in TV drama. Paper presented to American Psychological Association symposium entitled Children's processing of information from television. New York, September, 1979.

5. Comstock, G., Chaffee, S., Katzman, N., McCombs, M., and Roberts, D. *Television and human behavior.* New York: Columbia University Press, 1978.

6. Dorr, A. When I was a child, I thought as a child. Unpublished manuscript, Harvard, 1978.

7. Hawkins, R. The dimensional structure of children's perceptions of television reality. *Communication Research,* 1977, 3, 299-320.

8. Lyle, J. and Hoffman, H. Children's use of television and other media. In G.A. Comstock, A.A. Rubinstein and J.P. Murray (eds) *Television and social behavior vol. 5.* Washington, D.C.: Government Printing Office, 1972.

9. Roberts, D.F. Children and communication: a developmental approach. In I. de S. Pool, F.W. Frey, W. Schramm, N. Maccoby, and E. Parker (eds.) *Handbook of communication.* Chicago: Randy McNally, 1973.

10. Roberts, D.F. Testimony before the Federal Trade Commission: Child advertising hearings. Washington, D.C., 1979.

11. Salomon, G. *Interaction of media, cognition and learning.* Washington, D.C.: Josey-Bass, 1979.

12. Schramm, W., Lyle, J. and Parker, E. *Television in the lives of our children, Stanford, Calif.: Stanford University Press, 1961.*

13. Tada, T. Image Cognition: A developmental approach. Japanese Studies of Broadcasting, 1969, 7, 105-74.

14. Ward, S., Wackman, D.B. and Wartella, E. *How children learn to buy.* Beverly Hills: Sage, 1977.

15. Wartella, E. Children and television: The development of the child's understanding of the medium. *Television programming for children: A report of the children's television task force vol. 5,* Washington, D.C. Federal Communication Commission, 1979.

16. Wartella, E. and Alexander, A. Children's organization of impressions of television characters. Paper presented to the International Communication Association Convention, Chicago, Illinois, April, 1978.

17. Wartella, E. Alexander, A. and Lemish, D. Mass media environment of children. *American Behavioral Scientist,* 1979, *23* (no. 1), 33-52.

Support For A Skillful Audience

Donald E. Agostino

INSTITUTIONAL FOUNDATION FOR RECEIVERSHIP SKILLS

The development of curricular programs to develop critical receivership skills (CRS) involves the institutions of the family, classroom teacher, the consumer movement and the television industry. Each has a stake in the quality of viewing of television. An interdependent partnership of these groups which operates outside the classroom, I propose, is required to support in-school CRS programs.

Without the active participation of parents, schools, consumer groups and the television industry, the benefits of classroom programs teaching critical viewing will not last. The many countervailing influences in the child's daily experience will erode individual progress. However, sustained reinforcement from each of the four groups jointly engaged in projects that reach beyond the classroom will keep established skills of visual literacy from dissipating.

Donald E. Agostino, Ph.D. is a member of the Institute for Communication Research and Assistant Professor in the Department of Telecommunications Indiana University.

The analogy of nutrition is useful. To improve diet, it is not enough to formally teach good nutrition, healthful foods must be made readily available and people must be motivated to improve their eating habits.

The institutions of family, teacher, consumer activities and industry are at the center of many contemporary issues and each is legitimately preoccupied with individual challenges. And they have not been notably effective in past interaction. However, the first requirement for an environment supportive of CRS programs is motivation of fuller, more trusting cooperation among these four powerful institutions.

A second requirement is that CRS programs both utilize the functions and strengths of the four groups and accept the real limits and conditions of each.

The Family

Though troubled by economic and social conditions, family life remains the first experience of fundamental dispositions and values. In the family most children first learn what to do with their attention. Family values become the criteria of what is worth attending to within direct and mediated experience. So the family, specifically parents, are essential partners in development of the individual's virtues we call critical receivership or viewing skills—specifically the reflective and informed judgement in the choice and active viewing of television. Such choice is both formative and reflective of the values impressed by family life, values of self-image, of position and role in the concentric communities of family, peers neighbors, church, community and culture. Put another way, a student's habits of media use are strongly formed by family and are unlikely to change without family cooperation (6).

Teachers

Unlike parents, classroom teachers generally know how to use popular television programs as a basis for instructive discussion or the exercise of students' thinking and language skills. Many recognize CRS activities as both substantive exercises of basic learning skills and effective instruction because popular television provides students with a common, appealing story experience.

Though curriculum objectives and the art of teaching itself are value laden, teachers dislike any classroom program aimed at valuistic results. In the case of CRS, however, the curriculum proposes for the student purposeful choice, monitoring and appreciating of television use on the basis of personal rather than imposed values. Therefore, CRS development helps the student order and internalize his or her own values, and helps the student understand the entertainment and information aspects of our social system. This understanding liberates intuition and intellect. For the teacher, then, by experience and design, a case can be made that CRS instruction fits at the core of a traditional curriculum.

Consumer Groups

National consumer groups and local coalitions have focused the attention of broadcasters and regulators on some of the more jarring abuses and omissions of the industry, and have been successful in cajoling broadcasters to more responsive programming. More importantly, these consumer groups swung attention to the critical issue, how through the cooperation of producers and the intervention of schools and parents, the viewing experience can be constructive.

The Television Industry

There can be little doubt that television is a source of considerable pleasure in the lives of Americans. The typical viewer devotes relatively large amounts of time to television (1,2). Viewers express general satisfaction with the medium: a majority indicate they watch something worthwhile daily (4). A small percentage indicate strong *negative* feeling about television, yet these usually specify their complaint by saying they wish there were more programs like their favorite (7).

The art of television is to maintain this contentment, no matter how fleeting or superficial the benefit. The networks, the central programming authority in broadcasting, are singly successful at developing programming of broad, sustained appeal. Within this limited principle of mass popularity and while feeding the viewers' voracious appetite for entertainment, networks have contributed just about everything that makes television valued in the family or classroom. *Roots,* the ratings winner of 25 years of programming, was discussed by families, made homework by classroom teachers and the model for similar program series. *A Woman Called Moses* provided a stunning historical role model of individual character and leadership in a year burdened with newspaper essays on the need for political leadership.

ABC After-School Specials are in their eighth season. This year CBS will present 28 special children's programs; NBC is running "How to Watch TV" public service announcements. News segments and less advertising within children's programming are other improvements from the networks responding to concern and pressure by parents, consumer and professional groups. Much more can be done, of course, but positive change has been effected by the marketplace interaction of these concerned groups.

Benefits of Institutional Cooperation

Benefits of interdependent effort and cooperation among all four of these groups will give scope beyond the classroom to receivership skills programs. It will make sure that the benefits of the program reach the information poor as well as the information rich. Further, cooperative programs do not need to wait for resolution of the research questions dealing with the relationship between viewer disposition and program content. The causal connections between viewing competency and media content are still emerging. Clearly the content of mediated experience helps determine personal characteristics of the viewer, and the capabilities of the viewer condition the content of the viewing experience. Without sorting out which is horse and which is cart on the many avenues of this issue, receivership skills programs can, with partnership of consumer activists and the television industry, simultaneously improve both skills of viewers and the materials for viewing.

Finally, this coordinated approach, though difficult and dependent on cross-institutional communication, does not separate either the student or television from the contextual systems of society. It does not demand ingenuity, service and risk from broadcasters and neglect to ask parents, teachers, activists and scholars to contribute the same. And such an approach does not depend on government regulation.

SPECIFIC INITIATIVES

The task of policy is not only to enunciate general goals, but also specific means. With a broadened purpose; four groups of willing workers and several preconditions, what are the specific objectives? There are five practical activities which I submit for your refinement. I believe they are manageable, acceptable to each of the four groups and will generate benefits worth the effort to construct them.

1. Involve Institutions in Local Television

The first is the involvement of local institutions in local television production. The Carnegie Commission (5) once again pointed out that the instructional resources of television are still undeveloped, a theme repeated since the Fifties. A fresh approach to this problem I suggest, is the entry of other informational community institutions into local television. Art museums, theatre groups, science and technology centers, human service groups such as 4-H or Boy Scouts whose function is to form or inform, should be using television, the best developed information system ever devised.

The King Tut and Pompeii exhibits drew record crowds and swelled the museum coffers because of media attention and promotion. Broadway shows such as "Chorus Line" sell tickets not on the strength of critical reviews but on the "pizzazz" of their 30-second television spots. Public institutions need to learn this lesson about television's power. Is it sensible that curators of vast physical and intellectual treasure such as the Smithsonian Institution share this wealth with 100 thousand magazine readers while the nation of 220 million watches television? Broadcasting and the new television technologies are opportunities well suited to these institutions, large and small. For their own and the viewers' good, they need to get onto television.

2. Prime-time Series

Second, I propose a prime-time series for purposive television programming. The ratings success of the magazine shows *60 Minutes* and *20/20* indicate the networks' ability to produce new program forms and the responsiveness of the mass audience. By purposive I do not mean heavily didactic as *Connections* the current PBS series on technology. Nor do I mean shows such as *Nova* or *Masterpiece Theatre* which serve their small, predisposed audiences but attract inconsequential shares of the 50 million households which nightly turn to television.

A captivating television series well written for a general audience, tightly produced, promoted heavily as part of the prime-time schedule, boldly scheduled and given time to establish itself is certainly not beyond the creative and financial resources of the industry. Such a series would not seem to be of any greater risk in the network wars than some of the sitcoms introduced last October, and it would provide a needed starting point for a coalition of parents, teachers and consumer groups.

3. Language Programming

Purposive programs of wide appeal and distribution are needed for all age groups. A subject area of major importance worth priority concern is, I believe, foreign languages. Such programming, not necessarily by broadcast networking, is my third proposal. Students and all Americans are tongue-tied in an increasingly international world. Only nine per cent of college students are enrolled in foreign language courses. Only four per cent of public high-school graduates have studied a foreign language for more than two years (3). Our industrialized culture needs language skills as critically as engineering skills. And our schools will not be able to train bilingual citizens without a massive media-based program. Foreign programming in its original language can be made available in this country via the new delivery systems of cable, satellite-relay and direct marketing or exchanging of home video software. Further, a two-track audio system, simulcasting, or separate cable channels such as the Spanish network should be used to distribute some popular American shows in bi-lingual versions.

4. Program Information

More meaningful information, more communication is needed about television programs. The announcements and materials of the Television Information Office are helpful, and Prime Time School Television is a major contribution, but more is needed. Somewhere, whether on-air, in newspaper listings or by one of the new slick magazines about television, there should be full and thoughtful information about a variety of programs, readily available information which will aid viewers, parents and teachers in terms of critical viewing interaction.

5. New Technology

Finally, educators should hasten into the new video medium of videodisc software. Though for thirty years classroom teachers have been deafened by the overpromises of audio-visual systems developers, the video disc may finally bring those promises to fruition. Disc players are inexpensive and standardized. Software is extremely cheap to produce at about $5 retail per 2-hour disc with production break-even at 10,000 units. It gives a detailed color image in any mode from fixed frame to three times real speed in forward or reverse. It has 54,000 individually addressable frames on a side, so for instance, the history of Western sculpture could be represented on one disc. Neither first graders, AV librarians nor the U.S. Postal system can hurt the indestructible disc. And it is suitable for interactive, branching instructional materials. Chevrolet dealers use this video information system for sales and training presentations, parts lists and repair procedures.

The disc system, at much less cost than video cassette recording, gives the viewer control over television programming, one of the purposes and rewards of achieving critical viewing skills.

Conclusion

These five are ambitious proposals, I grant you. And it can be argued that such diversification of effort may stifle the success of the classroom efforts. With a working partnership of the four major sectors, however, in projects such as these which go beyond the classroom progress will be quicker and more permanent in terms of both the quality of programming and the quality of viewing.

Recall the anchorman in the movie *Network* surrounded by cameras, monitors, cue-cards? He pleads with the live audience in the limbo beyond the stage lighting: "You're beginning to think the tube is reality and that your own lives are unreal. In God's name you people are the real thing. *We are the illusions.*" The audience, waiting for an exciting prophecy, doesn't even listen. They are too far gone to recognize that the prophecy has been given and fulfilled. The anchorman is right. But we are critically different than that audience. And together—parents, teachers, activists and industry—we can teach the next generation to correctly discriminate which is illusion and which is reality, and to enjoy the wise use of each.

REFERENCES

1. A.C. Nielsen Company. *The Television audience.* Northbrook, Illinois: A.C. Nielsen Company, 1977.

2. Bower, T. *Television and the Public.* New York: Holt, Rinehart, and Winston, 1973

3. Fulbright, J. My turn. *Newsweek,* July 30, 1979.

4. LoSciuto, A. A national inventory of television viewing behavior. In E.A. Rubinstein, G.A. Comstock, and J.P. Murray (eds.), *Television and Social Behavior Vol 4.: Television in day-to-day life: Patterns of use.* Washington, D.C.: Government Printing Office, 1972, pp. 33-36.

5. *A public trust: The report of the Carnegie Commission on the future of public broadcasting.* New York: Bantam Books, 1979.

6. Rosengren, K.E. and Wendahl. S. Media panel: A presentation of a program. *Media panel.* Lunds University, No. 4, 1978.

7. Steiner, G. *The people look at television.* New York: Alfred A. Knopf, 1963.

Beyond 1984

Peggy Charren

INTRODUCTION

Beyond 1984. Orwell said it! "The instrument could be dimmed" he wrote, "but there was no way of shutting it off."

Today, we watch television. In Orwell's tomorrow, television watches us. TV today is controlled by Big Business. Orwell's control was Big Brother. Economic power vs. political domination.

The catalog of horrors that Orwell presented to the world as a warning reminds us that there could be worse telecommunications problems than those that concern us today.

Just as there are worse problems for children than television. For example, in this International Year of the Child, there are 17 1/2 million American children and young people who live in dire poverty. Ten percent have no regular source of medical care - 20 million have never seen a dentist. One million are victims of child abuse. And every year, one million young Americans run away from home.

Then why, faced with concerns of such serious nature, are we considering the issues of children and television? It is because those who care, those who

---

Peggy Charren is President of Action for Children's Television. This paper was the luncheon address at the first day of the conference.

are entrusted with a child's welfare, recognize the tremendous impact and influence that television has upon children.

And, of course, it is not just the child audience that is influenced by TV. Studies and polls have indicated that Americans get the bulk of their information from television, thus fulfilling the most dismal expectations of the medium's critics.

But the TV connection is most firmly in place for children. For they are the audience that spends between 25 and 30 hours a week watching television. The ease with which we toss about such figures is deceptive because the numbers must startle us when we realize how they add up. By the time children reach the age of 18, they will have spent approximately 15,000 hours watching TV; more time than they will spend at any other activity except sleep; more time than they will spend in school.

The sum of all those hours and days and years, with no time off for vacations or weekends, represents more than just figures, of course. If adults are getting their information from television, certainly, so are children. And in some surprising ways. For TV is the most powerful teaching machine the world has ever known. And the messages from the medium are present in every commercial and every program the children see. Information? Education? Children are learning not just how to study the stars or canvass the seas but they're also learning - as a 3rd grade class so recently displayed that the way to spell RELIEF is R-O-L-A-I-D-S. And while only one half of the world's adults can identify their national leaders, 90 percent of American three-year-olds recognize Fred Flintstone.

The world children watch on TV is peopled primarily by white American males, age 18 to 35. Women are more often witches than workers; blacks sing and play basketball; Asians are villains; and the elderly are victims. These portrayals, these stereotypes are being perpetuated daily in our own homes, upon our own children. Television, which has a unique capacity to affect and influence attitudes, is a school of sociology, instructing children about what they may expect from others and what goals to set for themselves.

A litany of names from the new network children's season will give some idea of the creativity and humanity that fills the airwaves on Saturday morning:

Godzilla and his nephew Godzooky
Fangface and his cousin Fangpuss
Scooby Doo and his nephew Scrappy Doo
Yukk
Hubba Bubba
Suckerman
and Plasticman's Hawaiian sidekick, Hula-Hula,
a derogatory stereotype that would make even Archie
Bunker squirm.

If this suggests to you that the special needs of the child audience are not being served by commercial television, you are right. This is not a matter of personal opinion or generalized theory; it is now—since last Tuesday, October 30—a matter of documentation. For on that day, the Federal Communications Commission issued its long-awaited staff report on its inquiry into children's television. And they found the product wanting. Specifically, the 800 page FCC report contends that broadcasters have failed to serve "the unique needs of the child audience" as directed in the 1974 Commission guidelines for children's television.

Pointing out that educating our children can provide immeasurable benefits to society as a whole, the FCC staff took broadcasters to task for not producing enough children's programs designed to inform and educate. The staff recommended that the FCC impose minimum educational program requirements on all stations (seven and one-half hours Monday through Friday), echoing ACT's long-held position that *per se* rules are the only way to guarantee that broadcasters comply with Commission policy. A second FCC recommendation is increased funding for PBS children's programs, a suggestion strongly seconded by ACT, a long-time supporter of the Public Broadcasting alternative.

They also recommended that the FCC might encourage children's educational programming by permitting commercials to be aired during publicly funded programs, an alarming notion flies in the face of the Commission's long-stated policy against overcommercialization on children's television, as well as evidence in the FCC staff report itself that young children do not fully understand televised messages. As the evidence that TV ads deceive kids piles up just across town at the FTC, it is incredible that the FCC could even consider using increased educational programming, however badly needed, to justify commercial exploitation of America's most vulnerable audience.

In side-stepping the issues of advertising targeted to children, the FCC is avoiding a question that cannot be ignored by anyone else who watches television. Children see over 20,000 commercials a year and advertisers spend over 600 million dollars per year selling to children on TV. Children are learning from these advertising messages. They are learning that if they own a certain toy they will be happy and have friends. They are learning that if they will eat sugary foods they can be healthy and strong. What they are *not* learning is that 60 percent of all foods advertised to children conflict with the Surgeon General's report recommending that Americans reduce sugar consumption. The heavily sweetened, attractively packaged foods that are sold to children in animated, appealing TV ads are also in conflict with the nutritional goals established by the Senate Select Committee on Nutrition and Human Needs.

That is the situation today. For tomorrow, for 1984 and beyond, I want to make three predictions.

First, there will still be economic control of television in 1984. Although

Big Business is preferable to Big Brother, there are still problems. One is the lack of diversity. All too often, we get a cookie-cutter product on television, easy to duplicate, profitable to manufacture. The reasons for this are clear. The commercial broadcasters are playing for serious stakes in a numbers game where only one number counts. Number One. The ratings determine revenues; they determine supremacy. This is an industry where the dominant thinking is to avoid risks...whose slogan might be "spinoffs are safer." This is an industry that minimizes its public commitment to inform and entertain and reaps the benefits of its primary purpose: to make money.

Other problems of economic control? A business that is operated by a particular group reflects the culture of that group. White, middle-class males run the shop. White, middle-class males are the medium's dominant characters. Equal employment opportunities are a way for women and minorities to get to a point where they too are running the shop so that their views, their ideas and energies can be represented.

In tomorrow's world of alternate technologies, is it not likely that we will still find telecommunications a business? Though there will be multiple channels, though narrowcasting will provide a broadcasting alternative, it could mean, quite simply, that more is not necessarily better...that more offerings will not indicate more choice. For mediocrity can be programmed on multiple channels as well as on individual networks. When we speak of diversity as a positive goal for television, we are not just talking about numbers. We are talking about quality.

My second prediction: That the more things change, the more they stay the same. Children will still be watching too much television.

And they watch a lot now. Not only do they watch a lot, they're watching more than they did before. And why not? Television is easy; it's available—98 percent of all American homes have it—and it's pleasant. A soporific for the senses.

But faster than we can comprehend, technology is shaping a vast new future for television. Diversity, choice and far-reaching possibilities are just ahead of us. Here are just a few of the new choices technology is providing:

Television channel selections are now multiplying five or six stations to 20 or more viewing choices. Cable TV will offer 40 channels on a single cable or 80 channels on a dual cable system.

Video cassette recorders give parents greater choice in selecting the best programs and choosing appropriate times for their children to view these programs. Video recorders with increased capabilities are moving into mass production at lower costs to consumers.

Video discs will allow us to purchase or rent programs of our own choice. Or, we can soon borrow from local libraries hundreds or even thousands of programs—14th century art, the history of dance, children's classics, the possibilities are endless.

The television set itself will be transformed with two-way transmission and home computer systems.

And according to Richard Mott, vice president of the Public Service Satellite Consortium, more than half the school systems will be using electronically broadcast material produced by educational cooperatives. Technology will make us, if anything, more—not less—dependent on the electronic transmission of information.

With the potential for more active viewer participation on the part of both adults and children, we can hope that more critical viewing will occur. Consciousness can be raised to the point where televised depictions of racism, sexism, ageism will no longer be tolerated. And perhaps the number of viewing hours a week will decline at least a little bit. Perhaps.

My third prediction. There will still be advertising to children on television. 1984 is just five years away and no image of Elysian Fields appears in my crystal ball. The expensive toys, the wrong foods will still appear on commercial television to entice new generations of young Americans. Will there be advertising on cable television? It is conceivable that a half hour commercial for children emanating from a toy store will be in the wave of the future. There could be advertising on video discs, even though the disc is assigned for homework. Instead of the millenium, we will still have a medium that sells children products they don't need at prices they can't afford.

Unless. Unless procedures currently underway can advance, bringing about needed change. Right now, in 1979, the children's television advertising issue is being deliberated by the Federal Trade Commission. And at the current rate of progress, it could still be tied up in the courts in 1984, if not 2001. The proposals before the FTC represent a very modest step. They will not *ban* sugar; they will not even prohibit the advertisement of sugared foods. The rules merely attempt to prevent excessive exposure of children to televised ads for a super sweet diet.

More than ten years of child advocacy in the television industry has taught us that broadcasting's primary concern is its bottom line. ACT and numerous other organizations involved with children know that the bottom line for the future of American society is the health, education and welfare of the nation's 40 million children.

Certainly broadcasters are not responsible for the welfare of children, but they do have a responsibility in the area of health and education. They should not make the rearing of a healthy, happy child more difficult for parents and physicians. Every day, commercial television violates the first principle of medicine, to "first do no harm," and persists in acting as though no body of knowledge exists about the developmental needs and the special hazards of childhood.

The long range interest of the society is never fully consistent with the short range budgets and objectives of the professional managers of our communications systems. The actions of the broadcasting and advertising industries over the past ten years prove that self-regulation alone will not correct abuses.

It took continuous effort over a five-year period and a consent order from the Federal Trade Commission to stop the selling directly to young children of candy coated pills.

It took five years of rulemaking at the Federal Communications Commission to reduce the advertising minutes on children's programs, and the National Association of Broadcasters' Code still permits more ads per hour to children than to adults on prime time.

Corporate executives are rewarded and promoted as a function of short range profitability. That is why it is essential that everyone who cares about children support the current rulemakings on children's television at the FCC and the FTC. A fair hearing of the issues and a careful consideration of solutions and strategies by these two agencies could mean a healthier and happier 1984 for children and their families.

Children and Television: A Legislator's Perspective

Congressman Marc Lincoln Marks

INTRODUCTION

The impact of television on children and society clearly is an important subject. While scholars have different opinions about the psychological and sociological consequences of watching television, the importance of television in the everyday life of children is readily apparent.

Anyone listening to and watching children at play undoubtedly finds them imitating characters such as Superman, the Incredible Hulk, and CHIPS. Spin-off from TV are reflected in children's toys and even in the clothes children wear. There must be a T-shirt for almost every major TV character. Last Halloween I noticed that while we had some creative creature visitors, we also had a lot of Star Wars and Disney characters. It is sad to think that the only things children might "play at being" are TV characters.

More importantly, we are becoming increasingly aware that television is not merely entertainment, and its impact is not limited simply to providing children with subjects for play or interesting T-shirts. We know television helps shape perceptions of reality and defines for us who and what is good and bad. Values conveyed in fiction are particularly important since this

---

Marc Lincoln Marks is a member of the U.S. House of Representatives from Pennsylvania. He wishes to acknowledge the assistance of his legislative assistant, Beverly Andrews, for her aid in preparing this paper.

format disarms viewers' alertness to value biases and stereotypes. Unfortunately, many viewers appear to accept the simplified statements and cliches transmitted by popular culture as valid. And certainly, it is not only kids who accept these messages as valid. As I recall reading, about 250,000 letters, most containing requests for medical advice, were sent to Marcus Welby, M.D.

Responsibility for Programming

I would today like to address the question of who should bear responsibility for television programming. In particular, what should be the role of Congress and government agencies relative to the role of parents, schools, and broadcasters in television programming? I say "relative" because I firmly believe that broadcasting is a *shared* responsibility. Yet, it is important to delineate spheres of responsibility. I think this is particularly true with regard to government involvement.

In determining spheres of responsibility, I find it useful to distinguish between two types of effects of television that have raised concerns. One effect is that of merely *watching* television irrespective of what is being watched. The other, is the effect of the *content* of television programs. I would like to discuss these in turn.

Mindless Viewing

The mere activity—or more accurately, the inactivity—of watching television is alone a cause for concern. The image of the passive viewer who becomes a mere "knob jockey" instead of an active participant and the depiction of television as the "plug-in-drug" portray in a lucid manner the negative aspects of viewing. The responsibility for the amount of time a child spends watching television clearly lies with parents—not broadcasters not schools, and certainly not the government. Here, the solution, "turn off the set," is appropriate.

Turning off the set, however, is not the solution, and indeed in my opinion is not even an appropriate response, to concerns raised about the content of television programs.

According to the law—the Communications Act of 1934—broadcasters are required to obtain from the Federal Communications Commission (FCC) a license to broadcast over the airwaves. These airwaves are a public resource and, in exchange for the very profitable privilege of using this resource, broadcasters are obligated to act as public trustees and to program according to the needs, interests, and concerns of those in the community they are licensed to serve.

Should the community too often find that its programming needs are not met, the solution to this poor programming is not to turn off the set. The public is not obliged to accommodate broadcasters. The public has a right to demand quality programs, and broadcasters are obligated to respond. If not, their licenses should be challenged.

The responsibility for programming should rest with broadcasters and those for whom they are supposed to be programming—the community, not the advertisers. Pressures for programs and guidelines for programs that serve the needs of the community should come from the community, not from the FCC or Congress. The primary focus of attention for parents and teachers should be on getting good programs on the air, rather that compensating for or ameliorating the effects of bad programs. While I think teaching critical viewing skills is important, I do not think this effort should take precedence over efforts to get good programs on the air in the first place.

THE FEDERAL ROLE

Where community actions are not effective in bringing about broadcaster responsiveness, the agency responsible for licensing broadcasters, the FCC, must come into play. This essentially is what happened with respect to children's programming, which is why, in 1974, the Commission issued a set of guidelines for children's programming and advertising. The Commission found in its Second Inquiry, issued in October, 1979, that broadcasters have not voluntarily adhered to most of these guidelines. This lack of compliance generally is attributed to the fact that broadcasters have no economic incentive to air children's shows because children do not constitute a significant market for advertisers. A prime-time adult program advertising minute can sell for a significantly greater amount than one minute in a children's program. Given this economic base of television, it is not hard to understand why there is little children's programming and why what there is appears at times for which no other audience is likely.

When both community pressure and voluntary compliance with government guidelines fail to bring about desired programming, then what course of action should those charged with regulating the industry in the public interest—the FCC—take? What should the government's role in programming be? What can be done legislatively?

Clearly, the government cannot and should not regulate content. Section 326 of the 1934 Act specifically precludes the FCC from censoring or interfering with broadcasters' freedom of expression. The FCC cannot infringe upon first amendment principles.

At the same time, the FCC is legally mandated to arbitrate between the broadcaster's freedom of expression and the community's right to be served by the licensee. Hence the dilemma: whenever the FCC tries to require that broadcasters meet certain types of programming needs in response to the community, broadcasters charge the FCC with censorship.

A recent example of this is the proposal of the FCC's Children's Television Task Force which maintains that the Commission should mandate all licensees to air weekly five hours of pre-school educational/instructional programming between 8 a.m. and 8 p.m. on weekdays and two and one-half hours of such programming for school age children.

There are precedents—equal time for political candidates, the fairness doctrine for public issues, and FCC minimum percentage guidelines for informational, nonentertainment, and local programming—for requiring broadcasters to present a specific type of program content. There is also the Supreme Court's decision in *Red Lion Broadcasting Company* v. *Federal Communications Commission,* 395 U.S. 367 (1969), stating that it is the right of the viewing and listening public, and not the right of broadcasters, which is paramount. While I support these general measures, I am ambivalent about establishing a precedent for mandating specific types of programs for a specific category of viewers. I would prefer the FCC to deal much more harshly with broadcasters at license renewal time if the licensee has repeatedly failed to satisfy community demands or standards such as those proposed by the Children's Television Task Force, than having the FCC impose "x" type of programs for "x" type of viewers for "x" hours of the week during "x" time periods.

ECONOMIC INCENTIVES

Options other than community pressure, stricter evaluations of performance at license renewal time, and mandatory programming requirements have been suggested. Rather than quantifying program requirements by time, the possibility of quantifying by dollars, might be explored. For example, a certain percentage of a station's overall operating budget might be required to be devoted to certain types of programming. While this tack is less subject to charges of censorship, broadcasters still object to interference in their business.

Providing economic incentives to broadcasters for airing children's programs also has been suggested. Recognizing the limitations of an advertiser—supported broadcasting system, which excludes the program needs of those who do not constitute a market advertisers care to reach, the federal government has sought to compensate by allocating funds for the production of programs. This currently is done through the Corporation for Public Broadcasting and through the Office of Education. But providing financial assistance for the *production* of programs is only one facet of the problem; programs also must be *distributed.* Public television, however, does not yet reach a large percentage of TV viewers. While government-funded programs are offered free to commercial stations, commercial broadcasters still have little incentive to air them since Congress does not permit commercials with publicly funded shows. The basis for this prohibition is the belief that broadcasters should not be able to profit from programs financed by taxpayers.

A more important and promising option is contained in the continuing development of technology which will provide us with a number of alternative distribution systems. As cable, fiber optics, and satellite technology develop, we can look forward to a much, much larger offering of programs from a number of hopefully diverse sources. It is expected that these new sources will shape their products to appeal to specialized tastes as a means of obtaining a share of the market. Proceeding on this theory, some observers feel that with the development of new technologies, "broadcasting" will shift to "narrowcasting" and the needs of specialized audiences will be met as a function of the marketplace rendering federal regulation unnecessary.

CONCLUSIONS

In the meantime, the question of how to require broadcasters to meet programming needs identified by the public without touching off concerns of federal censorship continues to pose a dilemma for the FCC and for legislators. Given these concerns, federal government mandating specific types of programming for specific audiences does not seem the most appropriate form of federal responsibility.

This does not mean, however, that bad programming must merely be accepted and that parents and teachers must therefore expend a lot of resources in compensating for these effects. Broadcasters, after all, have a legal obligation to serve the public interest, and the way this obligation has or has not been met should be carefully reviewed and enforced at the time of the broadcaster's license renewal. The community should play a vital role in this process, and the law and the procedures by which it is carried out should fully allow the community to play this vital role.

SECTION II

Critical Viewing Skills Projects for the Elementary Level

The following section reports on a few projects which have attempted to provide curriculum content for the lower elementary level in the area of critical receivership skills. The Idaho Falls project for grades three through six was conceived on the broadest scale of all the critical viewing projects reported at the Conference. It was a four year vertically integrated curriculum which put its emphasis on the analysis and evaluation of information and entertainment content. The other projects reported were more modular in design, intended to be added on or dropped into existing programs.

The A&R sessions strongly supported the notion that critical receivership skills curricula (CRS) needed to be a natural aspect of the total curriculum rather than a separate package. Only an integrated approach, the discussants argued, could provide the broad base necessary for dealing with the emotive and value-laden aspects of media content and the analytical skills which apply to all informational sources.

Conferees also argued that media based curricula need to show integration into the larger societal nest. There are shared responsibilities for dealing with the media among school, family, industry, activist groups and government. Only parents should regulate or guide children's choices. The school has the responsibility for teaching the language arts. These arts must be systematically expanded beyond their present print limits to include the aural and visual media. There is room throughout the curriculum to include every aspect of these media. Activist groups and government were seen as forces which could help modify the excesses of the marketplace. There was support for the industry, however. One conferee was roundly applauded for saying: "Let's put the emphasis on the positive experiences which can be gained from television rather than dwelling on the negative impact on T.V. All TV is not junk." The groups did call on the industry to assume more responsibility for quality and variety in programming at the same time realizing that it will take an enlightened public to make these services profitable.

The Way We See It:
A Program Design For Instruction
Of Critical Televiewing Skills

By N. Craig Ashton

INTRODUCTION

Educators in many areas are becoming aware of the increasing role that television is playing in our society and of the subsequent effects of this expanding communication medium on students. This recognition has, in part, been developed by an increasing call of action for educators to begin to teach students responsible televiewing skills. The call for public education to become involved in television training is attempting, in part, to be answered by the Idaho Falls School District through a federal Title IV-C curriculum innovation project. The project, entitled *The Way We See It,* is attempting to teach critical televiewing skills to students in Grades Three through Six. The program is unique, not only due to the age of the learner, but also because of the overall scope of the intervention, which attempts to develop critical thinking by teaching students to accurately understand, analyze and evaluate televised messages.

It is the purpose of this paper to explore the curriculum and intervention of this innovative project in relation to societal needs as well as student outcomes.

N. Craig Ashton is Coordinator of Federal Programs and Director of *The Way We See It* Project for the Idaho Falls School District No. 91, Idaho Falls, Idaho.

THE NEED FOR RECEIVERSHIP TRAINING

It has become an increasing note of concern on the part of school administrators that students appear to be spending less time in interpersonal communication with parents and the adult world. The problem is complex and not without a single cause or solution, as a variety of social forces may be contributing to the decrease of interpersonal communication with parents. One factor may actually be the lack of availability of parent with the growing trend for both parents to be entering the labor force. School as well may have generated some deterioration of communication through teaching methodologies which limit teacher-student interpersonal exchange. Society itself has contributed to the problem as it has moved from a structure of mutual dependence to a more individualistic society. It is also reasonable to assume that along with working parents, teaching patterns and a detached society that television may also be playing a significant role in the communication process.

Television viewing probably occupies far more time in the lives of children than does reading or interpersonal communication with parents. The amount of time spent in viewing television is a concern to the Idaho Falls School District for two reasons: 1) As a potential socializing agent, television program content requires young viewers to be prepared to respond critically and evaluatively and 2) students who are watching extensive amounts of television do not have the option of participating in alternative activities, only one of which is interpersonal communication.

Numerous agencies and social organizations have recently been criticizing the television industry concerning program content and specifically violence on television. It is important to address this issue since it was a basis of concern in the initial formation of the project. In essence, the effect of program content and television are currently inconclusive. We do, however, believe television programs are significant socializing influences for children and adults. If we do not understand this medium, we have no guidelines for interpreting and making discriminating judgments about programs. Those who finance television spend millions of dollars learning how to manipulate an audience. The audience needs competence in assessing the visual manipulation. It is the assumption of the project that content is a poor predictor of effect and that the receiver (student) should become the critical censor of program messages through an intelligent decision making process.

The project was written in response to this need. It has allowed the school district to begin training parents and students to use television as a positive communicational tool, and at the same time teach receivership skills. In essence, the need is responded to by teaching students to utilize television—not be used by it.

RATIONALE FOR EDUCATIONAL INVOLVEMENT IN RECEIVERSHIP TRAINING

Schools admittedly depend upon printed material as a basis for most of their formal instruction. The Idaho Falls School District is not reducing the utilization of printed material in its curriculum. However, it is aware that many skills can be taught through alternative communication media. One of these sources is television.

Students today are constantly being bombarded by messages from verbal, non-verbal, visual and written communication sources. The ability of the child to decode these messages, understand them, analyze them and determine their impact, is the essence of critical thinking. The development of critical thought has long been a goal of public education and specifically of the Idaho Falls School District. It is the assumption of the district that this thought process can be developed through the study of television as well as literature. This assumption is reinforced by drawing the conclusion that comprehension skills in a reading program can also be reinforced and extended through the analysis of television programming. The elements of literature (plot, setting, etc.) are also present in television programs, and the skills used in comprehension (determining theme, utilizing context clues, forming sequence and eliciting an awareness of cause and effect) can also be applied to the analysis of television.

The extension of basic skills in the curriculum is not the only advantage for utilization of television in education. The use of the medium itself has a recognized impact on the motivational state of the learner. Television in the classroom is not only a high interest instructional medium, but also provides a uniquely common instructional base.

The rationale for public educational involvement in receivership training appears to be sound when based upon the following factors:

1. The development of critical thinking can be enhanced through the study of television.
2. Basic comprehension skills can be extended and reinforced through analysis of television.
3. The use of the medium provides a high interest motivational approach with a common instructional base.
4. Receivership training allows students and parents to become more critical viewers. Hence, program selection is determined on the bias of intelligent decision making, rather than passive acceptance and manipulation.

CURRICULUM

The curriculum in the project has been scoped and sequenced by grade level in each of four major television content areas. The areas of instruction include commercials, entertainment, news, and personal uses. Each grade level has a teacher guide which includes objectives, background information, activities, materials and lesson development plans. Initial curriculum materials were developed by Dr. James Anderson from University of Utah and Dr. Milton Ploghoft from Ohio University on the basis of teacher formulated objectives. Since that time, teachers in the Idaho Falls School District have refined the materials and developed specific learning activities which are contained in the current teacher handbook, entitled *The Way We See It - A Guide For Teachers.*

The major instructional emphasis in each of four content areas will be discussed in this paper to help clarify the total scope of the critical televiewing project.

Commercials

The overall goal of the commercial unit is to provide students with concepts and skills that will enable them to analyze the persuasive messages of commercials, to discriminate between product and affective appeals and to become sensitive to the subtle persuaders. Activities to achieve this goal are different at each grade level. However, common objectives have been established for the overall content area. The objectives are as follows:

1. The student will identify different types of commercial messages in terms of their purposes.
2. The student will be able to identify various persuasive selling techniques that are used in TV commercials.
3. The student will be able to identify appropriate means to evaluate the performance of a product and to determine the validity of the advertised promises.
4. The student will be able to identify the motivating purposes behind product purchases.
5. The student will explain the place of television commercials in our current mercantile system and in the competitive, free enterprise economy of the United States.

Each of these objectives is covered at each grade level. However, major emphasis is placed upon the identification of persuasive selling techniques and studying motivating purposes behind product purchases. A description of the persuasive techniques which are emphasized in the project will be briefly explained in this paper.

Many times commercials attempt to set an affective state in the viewer so that a product will have a certain emotional appeal. An example of this type of appeal is evident in soda pop commercials where the product is often associated with friendship and goodtimes. Even the slogans suggest this inference with phrases like "Coke adds life." This technique is also used to promote long distance calls and is even used to suggest that a specific grocery store is a fun place to go.

Another form of persuasion is to try to associate a product with a famous personality. This associative technique is exemplified in a commercial which features both Henry Fonda and lifesavers. Although Henry Fonda may know very little about lifesavers, it is safe to assume that he is a successful salesman in his inferred endorsement of the product.

Production techniques in commercials also have a definite effect in the persuasion of children. This is dramatized by the film *Seeing Through Commercials* (Vision Films) which is an instructional tool in the project.

The end result of studying about persuasive elements in commercials is the development of the child's ability to become a more discriminating viewer. A student develops critical thinking skills by making judgments on the basis of fact and need, rather than manipulative persuasion. This process is reinforced by encouraging parents and children to discuss commercial appeals and techniques.

A specific culminating activity in the commercial curriculum enables teams of students to creatively plan, produce and film a television commercial based upon techniques and persuasive elements which have previously been learned. The commercials are then shown to parents in a series of group meetings where the effects of televiewing are discussed.

Entertainment

The overall goal of the entertainment unit is to provide students with analytical tools that will be useful in the evaluation of the content of entertainment programming. The project attempts to help prepare young viewers to identify value conflicts and to provide experiences in value clarification with the consideration of reasonable alternatives to problem solutions which are presented in television programs.

Again, specific objectives have been developed for the entertainment unit which are followed through at each grade level. The entertainment curriculum emphasis can be categorized in the following areas:

1. Students are made aware of the reasons and motivation for watching television.
2. Skills for determining the inherent value statements in entertainment programming are presented to students.
3. The development of comprehension and evaluation skills are taught through program analysis.

It is important that students become aware that individuals watch television for different reasons and that the motivation and receptiveness of the viewer directly affect the consequences of viewing. Students in the project are asked to examine their own motivation for watching in relation to their need states. One of the activities within the field of emphasis requires the students to go "cold turkey" without television for one weekend. The result is a *vivid* discussion concerning the psychological need for television, alternative activities and feelings about "withdrawal."

Television as a value agent has been researched and studied to determine the degree of imitative behavior that is elicited in children following exposure to television. Some studies have indicated that children's perceptions of the behavior of television characters are closely related to their own. The project accepts the rationale that a certain amount of imitative behavior is developed from television. The project does not address the issue of right or wrong values or acceptable and non-acceptable role models. However, instruction within the project does teach that values *are* present in programming and that most characters hold specific value systems which can be transmitted to students, either through social learning or a lack of perceived reality. It is the intent of the project to encourage parents to communicate with their children concerning the values that are expressed on television in relation to their own family value system. Again, television is used as a common ground for communication between parent and child.

Apart from the values which are explored at home, there are many social forces and situations which can be discussed at school and clarified through the study of television. An example is an examination of family structures or even the social stigma of stereotyping. This type of clarification concerning common social structures is an excellent teaching tool in the general social science curriculum and provides a good argument for infusion of television into existing curriculum.

The analysis of programming is a key element in the critical receivership curriculum. This activity centers around the viewing and treatment of at least six entertainment programs. The selected programs are a compilation of selected episodes from *Little House On The Prairie, White Shadow, Happy Days, Mork and Mindy, Eight Is Enough,* and *Taxi.* Each program is analyzed in terms of the following basic comprehension skills: main idea, sequence, understanding the character, cause and effect, predicting outcomes, inference, fact or opinion, context clues, sharing feelings, and summarizing. Value identification in the unit is achieved through group discussions at school and value clarification is encouraged through the parent component. The culminating step in the process is for the student to make a determination of the impact of the program on their lives. A sample lesson utilizing basic comprehension skills in the analysis of entertainment programming is included in the appendix. The lesson is based upon an episode from *Little House On The Prairie.* (The format for this analysis package is based upon the work of Educational Patterns Inc. TV Comprehension Program.)

News

Teaching strategies for the news content area are in contrast to those which are used in the entertainment and commercial units since news is studied in relation to other informational sources.

The collection and dissemination of news by television has become one of the major sources of information for students. It is likely that students will depend more upon the television for news than any other alternative information source. This dependence leads to the justification for teaching skills to help analyze the structure and content of television news.

The major curriculum emphasis is formulated into the following areas:
1. Students are taught to become aware of the limitations of television news (time constraints, selection of stories, editing, etc.).
2. Children are provided with an awareness of the capabilities of televised news programming (visual impact, concise summarized news items, collection of many stories in a short period of time, etc.).
3. Students practice skills in verifying television news through other information sources.
4. Parents and students are encouraged to communicate and share opinions about television news events.

A culminating activity in this content area allows groups of students to collect, edit, produce, present and film television news as a reinforcement to the skills which have previously been learned.

Personal Uses

This curriculum effort seeks to provide students the opportunity to learn about their own personal uses of television—what they like, how they watch, when they watch and why they watch.

The major activity in this area involves the maintenance of a personal viewing diary—then summarizing and analyzing the data which are collected.

INTERVENTION

Implementation of the overall project is attempting to be integrated into the existing Language Arts and Social Studies curriculums. This type of infusion is reflected in the study of non-verbal communication. Television can expand and reinforce this type of language arts study without supplanting existing curriculum. The instructional approach changes, but the concept to be learned remains the same. In the case of non-verbal communication, television enhances existing instructional technique.

This integration approach reduces the supplantive nature of the television curriculum, and is an answer to the common response from teachers that they do not have time to teach another "subject." All project activities, however, are not integrated with existing skills since there are many new concepts which must be taught. The overall process of instruction requires approximately one and a half hours of instructional time per week. This weekly approach is preferred. However, a consolidated fifty-four hour unit of instruction could be implemented utilizing the same materials.

PARENT COMPONENT

The inclusion of parents in the receivership curriculum is essential to increasing the impact of the program upon students. Parental involvement is seen as a method of increasing communications between children and parents. The ensuing interaction helps to defray any negative influences which may be presented in programming.

Research shows that 75 per cent of children's televiewing in the evening is watched in the presence of at least one parent and that 80 per cent of all children's viewing consists of adult prime time programming. These statistics would indicate that parental involvement is important in the process of developing receivership skills. Parents can help clarify and formulate values, which is an area that is difficult for public education to enter.

Parents are taught communication and value clarification skills in three ways. First, parents participate in evening discussion meetings where the effects of television on children are discussed. Second, training materials which correlate with curriculum content are sent home for use by parents. Thirdly, a series of six discussion guides are provided to parents. The guides are used by parents after viewing predetermined selected programs with their children. The guides offer suggested discussion questions and set a basis for communication between parent and child about the values expressed in the programs.

It is felt that through the implementation of this parental component that receivership skills can be reinforced and critical televiewing can be enhanced.

SUMMARY

The Idaho Falls School District has been able to successfully devise curriculum materials and implement a program of instruction in critical televiewing skills for elementary school students. The conclusions that can be drawn from this implementation are as follows:

1. The project was developed in response to a need revealed through the expanding role that television is playing in society. The school district is especially concerned about the extensive use of television by students, the possible effects of program content, and the ensuing lack of communication between parent and child.
2. The utilization of a receivership skills curriculum in public education can help enhance the development of critical thinking through the analysis of television.
3. The integration of the program into the regular educational curriculum can help expand basic comprehension skills and social studies concepts.
4. The television viewing habits of the selected population can be determined on the basis of intelligent decision making, rather than manipulative persuasion.
5. The effects of television program content can be molded through parental involvement in the televiewing process. Interpersonal communication between parent and child can be increased by utilizing television content as a common discussion base.

In essence, the project is trying to develop high cognitive receivership levels in students by teaching them to understand, analyze and evaluate televised messages. It is expected that the Idaho Falls project will generate new methodologies of instruction and can serve as a model for other school districts which may have similar concerns and needs. With the continued use and refinement of the television curriculum, the project hopes to improve, not only the receivership skills of students, but also strengthen the living learning environment of the individual, family and community.

Critical Television Viewing: A Public Television Station Reaches Out

By
Debbie Wasserman Bilowit

INTRODUCTION

How many times have we heard, "Children spend more time in front of a television set than do in a classroom?" By now that statement has almost become a cliche. Yet, it remains significant. For, if children are spending that much time watching television, it is a force to be reckoned with—not by ignoring it or condemning it as many advocates insist, but by finding ways to harness that force, by helping children to turn those viewing hours into active, thinking hours.

At PBS station WNET, in New York, we began working on this approach about ten years ago. At that time we were conducting workshops in schools to help teachers incorporate our daytime instructional television programs into the classroom. Teachers started to ask us how they could help their children become more active television viewers, how they as teachers could make use of the students' many hours of prime time viewing.

It sounded like a good idea to us. Children watch many hours of television, we thought. Let's help those teachers to turn those hours into a teaching resource—not just a few well-produced programs, not a special program here

---

Debbie Wasserman Bilowit is project director Critical Television Viewing Skills project for WNET/THIRTEEN, New York. The project is one of four funded by HEW.

and there, but every program, all of those hours. How? By adapting some standard learning skills to television, by teaching children analytical skills that they can practice every night when they watch television at home. For example, at some time, all children learn how to analyze a story according to its plot, conflict, setting, characters and theme. Those elements also exist in most of the television programs which children watch. Children who learn how to analyze television stories for plot, conflict, characters, setting and theme will not only be better able to understand TV situation comedies or dramas but also will be better able to understand, and enjoy, the books which they read.

CRITICAL TELEVISION VIEWING

The concept of helping children to understand television is now called "Critical Television Viewing" and, in various incarnations, it is being explored around the country. The term "Critical Television Viewing" has a different meaning for everyone. More often than not, that definition has to do with a person's individual concerns over television. Some people feel that there is too much violence on television, and for them critical television viewing means developing a sensitivity towards that violence. Some people feel that children watch too much television, and for them critical television viewing means knowing when to turn off the television set. And some people feel that the quality of television programs is poor, and for them critical television viewing means knowing how to evaluate them.

To us, critical television viewing is all of them and more. It includes pre-planned viewing schedules, an alertness to television's assets and drawbacks, an ability to evaluate quality, and most of all, an ability to make unique, well-informed judgments about television. Our task is not to persuade people to watch only TV programs that are "good" for them, but to help them develop the inner resources for setting their own personal criteria about what to watch and how to watch it. More specifically, critical television viewing skills are:
 * The ability to analyze what you see and hear on television;
 * The ability to evaluate what you have analyzed—for what is good about it, what is bad about it and how it relates to your life;
 * The ability to express that evaluation—through something you talk about, through something you may write, through something you may choose to read, or through the television programs you select to watch.

HOW DO YOU TEACH SOMEONE CRITICAL TELEVISION VIEWING SKILLS?

The WNET staff teaches critical television viewing through national workshops and print materials. Our approach is to concentrate on what the viewer sees and hears on television as opposed to developing background knowledge or technical expertise about television production. We approach critical television viewing the same way a language arts teacher might approach the analysis of a novel or poem: by looking at the piece which has been set before us. In our workshops and books we ask children and adults to analyze, evaluate and discuss some of the many different elements that they see and hear on television.

The following are some of those elements, each followed by questions which we ask people to consider. The first six elements are "literary" elements which children study in school when they learn how to analyze novels or short stories. The last four are "technical" elements which contribute to the impact of the program on the viewer.

LITERARY ELEMENTS

Characters

Who are the characters in the show? What do they look like? How do they dress? How do they move? How do they walk? How do they talk? Books use adjectives to describe characters. What adjectives would you use to describe the characters? Why did you choose those adjectives?

Setting

When and where did most of the action take place? This does not just mean major settings, but the minor settings, as well—some of the places where action might have taken place for only fifteen to thirty seconds. Why did the action take place there? Why do you suppose the director and set designer chose those locations? What do those locations look like? What are some of the details that you can remember from some of those locations?

Conflict

Who is clashing or disagreeing and what are they clashing or disagreeing about? This includes not only the major conflict in the story, but also the more subtle conflicts.

Plot

What happened in the story? How was the conflict resolved? What was the order of events, in detail?

Theme

What is one sentence that expresses the major theme or message of the story? What are the minor themes? How were these themes conveyed (dialogue, casting, plot?) Do you agree with those themes?

Logic

Was there anything in the story that did not make sense? Why do you suppose it did not make sense? (Because the story deals with a fantasy or supernatural situation, because the program must conform to certain time restrictions, because social convention discourages showing certain things on television, because the producer/director was careless.) How would the story have changed if everything made sense?

Overall Story Content

Did the story content interest you? Did you care about what was going to happen?

TECHNICAL ELEMENTS

Casting

Did the actors fit their roles? Who else might have played that role? Might the role have been played by someone older, younger, shorter, taller, of another race? How would different casting change the nature of the program? Would different casting contribute to or detract from the theme and the overall thrust of the program?

Make-up and Costume

Were the actors' costumes and make-up appropriate to the actors, the time the place and the situation? How might they have been different?

Music and Sound Effects

Was the choice of music appropriate for the scene, and did it make it better than it would have been without music? Were the sound effects believable? necessary? excessive? too sparse?

Special Effects

Did they look real? How do you think they were done? How else might they have been done? Were they necessary?

WHAT IS WNET'S CRITICAL VIEWING SKILLS PROJECT?

We have received two years of funding from the Department of Health, Education and Welfare to develop seven items. They are:

1. *A Student Work Text* A workbook and textbook combination for children in middle school grades which will teach them critical television viewing skills. The student book (published by Cambridge Book Co. is non-judgmental, relates critical viewing skills to language arts skills which are already being taught in the classroom, and it deals with generic skills that can be used with any television program. The curriculum in this book has been tested nationally and is now available for purchase.

2. *A Teacher's Annotated Edition to the student work text* This helps the teacher incorporate the student Work-A-Text into a classroom curriculum. It shows the teacher how critical viewing can be taught with television equipment and without equipment in the classroom.

3. *A Family Guide* An eight-page family guide which will help parents make more positive use of the programs which their children are already watching.

It recognizes that many parents do not watch television with their children.

4. *A Training Manual for Teacher Trainers*

5. *A Training Manual for Community Leaders* These training manuals are designed to help trainers work with either teachers or families to turn television viewing into positive experience. In the case of teacher trainers, the manuals will help trainers work with teachers to incorporate critical television viewing into a positive experience. In the case of teacher trainers, the manuals will help trainers work with teachers to incorporate critical community leaders work with families to make television viewing a good experience in the home and to help everybody to get more out of what they're watching.

6. *Training Sessions for Teacher Trainers*

7. *Training Sessions for Community Leaders* Besides doing national presentations, we have selected ten sites around the country, in which we will conduct one all-day training session with teacher trainers and one all-day training session with community leaders. We will also be working with the public television stations around the country as part of our training, and providing them with special Training Manuals.

DOES CRITICAL TELEVISION VIEWING WORK?

People are constantly asking us if children can actually learn generic critical television viewing skills which can be transferred to reading or writing. People are constantly asking us if children respond well to learning critical television viewing skills. The answer to both those questions is definitely yes. We tested our print materials and workshops around the country in the spring of 1979. Teachers, students and parents in Palo Alto (CA), Stanford (CT), Newark (NJ), Nashville (TN), Salt Lake City (UT) and Lafayette Parish (LA) used our guides and participated in workshops with our staff. In addition, we tested many of the activities in the guides before they were included. Here are some of the things we discovered:

1. Children can transfer their critical television viewing skills to books. Lynne Brenner Ganek, our Project Writer, is a classroom teacher on leave from the classroom. She visited her old school to test some activities with a sixth grade class. Before she began, she asked the students about books they were reading to see if they could tell her about the characters, setting, conflict, plot and theme. They couldn't. She then showed them a scene from All in the Family and talked about those elements as they related to the television program. They responded immediately. Lynne then began to talk with them about a book they had been reading in class in terms of character, setting, plot, conflict, and theme. And we found that most of the children were able to transfer that knowledge about TV

story elements immediately and without hesitation to books. Whereas before, they had been unable to discuss those books in literary terms, they now could.

2. Critical television viewing can be incorporated into the teachers' current classroom curricula. The teachers who used our materials in the classroom last spring told us how they incorporated them into their classes. Some of them taught one critical viewing concept a day—about fifteen minutes a day—and related those concepts, as they were appropriate to other subject areas. For instance, a teacher who taught a unit on news, might spend a few minutes each day doing those critical viewing activities which relate to television news. Some teachers spent one class period a week on critical television viewing. In come cases, they went through our work text in sequence; in other cases they chose chapters as they were relevant to other existing classroom subjects. One social studies teacher for instance used the chapter on television persuasion in conjunction with a unit on propaganda. And some teachers were able to arrange a special minicourse in critical television viewing which might last from one week to one semester. In those cases, the teachers related language arts or social studies skills as they were appropriate to what was being studied in critical television viewing.

3. Children can grasp critical television viewing skills fairly quickly. One activity which we conduct during our workshops involves observation. We show a scene from a television program to the participants and ask them to list all of the visual details they saw and the sounds that they heard. During one workshop in Nashville, Tennessee, the children became so enthusiastic about enumerating those details which they saw and heard, that we had to ask them to pause for a moment to give their parents and teachers time to speak. Another activity involves discussing the theme of a television program or commercial. In Palo Alto we explained the concept of "theme" to the children and then showed them a commercial for a breakfast cereal. We then asked the children "What is the theme of the commercial?" Naturally, at first they noted themes like, "Buy our cereal; our cereal tastes good"; but in a very brief amount of time, they were also adding other themes like, "women serve breakfast to men; breakfast can be fun; families should eat breakfast together." Time and time again, we discovered that children were quick to understand critical television viewing concepts and to relate them directly to television programs which they saw. We also found that children were eager to learn how to analyze television. This quick response led us to feel that perhaps we are not teaching the children anything new after all; we are simply helping them to organize and express their thoughts.

CONCLUDING THOUGHT

Critical Television Viewing is not a panacea. Its use will not suddenly turn everyone into incisive critical thinkers or avid readers. It can, however, help improve family communications, provide teachers with a classroom resource, and help children to make more informed decisions about their television viewing. We have been teaching children how to read books—how to analyze a novel or a poem and how to discuss the concepts presented in them. Now, let's teach them how to read television as well.

Teaching Elementary School Children
Critical Television Viewing Skills: An Evaluation

by Dorothy G. Singer, Diana M. Zuckerman and Jerome L. Singer

INTRODUCTION

Curricula have been developed over the years to teach children to read and understand a newspaper format: to recognize the masthead, and editorial, a book review, the sports section and special features and even how to use a newspaper as a resource to supplement classroom and textbook instruction (21). Radio has also been used to augment learning skills (18) and there have been lessons prepared by Instructional Television to teach children about "news" on television. There have been several attempts (1, 22, 24) to develop curricula to teach children about the nature of television. In May, 1979, the American Broadcasting Companies, Inc. awarded the Yale Family Television Research and Consultation Center a grant to develop and

---

Dorothy G. Singer is Professor of Psychology at the University of Bridgeport and Co-Director with Professor Jerome L. Singer of the Yale University Family Television Research and Consultation Center. Diana M. Zuckerman is a Postdoctoral Fellow at the Yale School of Medicine and was previously a Research Associate at the Psychology Department as project director for the study described herein. This study was supported by a grant from the American Broadcasting Companies, to Yale University. A version of this paper appears in *Journal of Communication*.

systematically assess the impact of such a television curriculum on third, fourth and fifth grade children. In September of 1979, the U.S. Office of Education also awarded contacts to four teams around the country to develop television curricula geared to specific age groups. Descriptions of these projects have been reported at various conferences and are currently in the preparation stages for dissemination.

The need for curricula designed for various age groups becomes apparent when we examine the literature describing the effects of TV on children. The most extensive research has been carried out on the effects of television violence on children and adults (20). More recent work by Lefkowitz, Eron, Huesmann and Walder (13), Belson (4), and Eron (9) demonstrated that the viewing of violent programs is a significant influence on the occurrence of aggressive behavior in elementary school aged and adolescent children. Singer and Singer (16,17) found that the amount of television viewing, particularly heavier viewing of action-adventure programs, was significantly related to childrens' aggressive acts in the nursery school.

In addition to the research on the effects of violent programs, there is a growing body of research on children's comprehension of television commercials. Systematic research by Ward, Wackman and Wartella (23) and Atkin (2) have demonstrated that children understand commercial messages more clearly as they get older, and they also become increasingly skeptical. A study by Galst and White (10) suggests that young children are clearly influenced by commercials to persuade their mothers to purchase TV advertised cereal products. Robertson & Rossiter (15) found that children's development in regard to understanding commercials was positively related to their parents' educational levels.

Disclaimers have presented problems to children as well. Such phrases as "assembly required", "each sold separately", and "batteries not included" are confusing to children. Research by Barry (3) and Liebert et al. (14) has shown that children understand disclaimers more accurately when they are worded more simply, e.g. "you have to put it together yourself."

Researchers have been concerned about television's impact on children's attitudes towards racial and sex roles. In her summary of studies on the mass media's presentation of sex-roles, Busby (5) found that television tends to depict women in relatively traditional and demeaning roles, and that female characters in detective shows tend to be victims or were depicted as less powerful than males. Sternglanz and Serbin examined popular children's shows (19) and found boys to be portrayed as more aggressive while girls were portrayed as less effective. Black characters are overrepresented in smaller, less important roles on television, (12), and as criminals and victims (11). In the late 1970's, most blacks were in situation comedies where they were depicted as members of poor, fatherless families. Many of the characters were unsuccessful, funloving, and used a constant stream of verbal put-downs directed towards other characters. Children's programs are still dominated by white characters in feature roles except for an occasional afternoon special such as NBC's *A piece of Cake* of CBS's *Joey and Redhawk*.

Besides these concerns about violence, commercials, race and sex stereotypes, there has been increasing consternation expressed by educators regarding televisions' impact on childrens' reading scores, on their ability to think critically and to attend or concentrate in school. The fast-pacing of television, the quick resolutions of problems, the interruptions of commercials during a story all pose potential problems in the classroom.

Collins (6,7) has suggested that young children have distorted comprehension of television programs as well as confusion concerning the sequence of events in a plot. Older children are more sophisticated about media presentations, but even third graders "pay attention to and remember fewer or different aspects of programs than adults would expect" (7, p. 199).

OBJECTIVES OF CRITICAL TV SKILLS PROJECT

The fact that the average elementary-school-aged child watches about 4 1/2 - 5 hours of television a day, suggested the two main goals of the present study, which were: (1) to develop, implement and evaluate a series of eight lesson plans that would teach third, fourth and fifth grade children to understand the television medium and to use their obvious interest in the medium in conjunction with reading, writing and discussion skills; (2) to evaluate the relationship between family background and children's viewing habits since past research suggests that children of these ages may be especially influenced by parental attitudes about television (8).

Thus the following study was designed to help children in these specific ways:

1. To understand the different types of television programs, such as news documentaries, variety, game shows, situation comedies, dramas, etc.
2. To understand that programs are created by writers, producers and directors and other personnel, and utilize actors and actresses as well as scenery and props.
3. To understand how television works in terms of simple electronics.
4. To learn what aspects of a program are real, and how fantasy or pretend elements are created for programs or commercials through camera techniques and special effects.
5. To learn about the purpose and types of commercials, including public service or political announcements.
6. To understand how television influences our feelings, ideas, selfconcept, and identification.
7. To become aware of television as a source of information about other people, countries, occupations; and how stereotypes are presented.

8. To examine violence on television and help children to be more critical of it; to become aware that we rarely see someone recovering from an act of violence on TV, or see the aggressor punished; to understand the distinction between verbal and physical aggression.

9. To encourage children to be aware of what they watch and how they can control their viewing habits, as well as how they can influence networks, producers, and local TV stations.

10. To use these lessons within a Language Arts framework so that children could gain experience in using correct grammar and spelling; writing letters; abstracting ideas; critical thinking; expressive language; oral discussion and reading.

PROCEDURE

We negotiated with the superintendent of a suburban school district and Board of Education in order to explain the purpose of the study and to obtain permission to carry it out. After principals of two elementary schools were consulted, and the teachers agreed to participate in the study, informed consent forms were distributed to parents of third, fourth and fifth graders in two schools matched for IQ, reading scores, ethnicity and socio-economic status. Parents of 134 (90.5 per cent) of the students in the experimental group and parents of 98 (73.1 per cent) of the students in the control group signed the forms agreeing to permit their children to participate as subjects. The mean age of the children was 9.5 years; fifth graders were slightly underrepresented. The children were somewhat above average in intelligence, with a mean IQ of 110 on the McGraw-Hill Intelligence Test. Their reading scores as measured by the McGraw-Hill Reading Test were about one year above average at each grade level. The modal and median parents' educational level was a bachelor's degree for the mothers and fathers of these children. The mean number of siblings was 1.6. Forty-three per cent of the families owned three or more television sets.

After pre-testing of experimental and control groups, the experimental condition consisted of eight lessons taught during a four-week period in October and November 1978. Two lessons were taught each week. Three months later, the experimental and control group were retested, and the control group was then exposed to the same lessons. The classroom teachers had been trained in four sessions in order to familiarize them with the lessons, and to present a model for teaching this new material. Two workshops were also held for the parents to acquaint them with the project.

The lessons included ten-minute videotapes narrated by an actress, which included videoclips from current TV shows, as well as original materials prepared in order to illustrate and elaborate the concepts to be taught. Lessons were about 40 minutes in duration, each highlighting a specific topic, with questions for discussion, vocabulary lists, activity sheets for classroom and homework, and suggested reference books. The children also received a booklet about television personnel and several illustrated articles about television production. The eight lesson topics were: Introduction to Television, Reality and Fantasy on Television, Camera Effects and Special Effects, Commercials and the Television Business, Identification with Television Characters, Stereotypes of Television, Violence and Aggression, and How Viewers can Influence Television.

RESULTS

Pretests, posttests, and follow-up tests included questions related to the eight topics and attitudes towards television. Pretesting took place in both experimental and control schools during the two weeks prior to the lessons and posttesting took place during the two weeks following the lessons in November. The February tests were the follow-up tests for the Experimental School (School A) and the second set of pretests for the Control School (School B). During the two week periods that the children completed pretests and posttests in the schools, their parents completed Family Television Viewing Records and Parent Information Forms.

Pretest and posttest responses were compared in order to determine the effects of the lessons on knowledge and attitudes towards television. The Control group (School B) was compared to the Experimental group (School A) in order to control for any changes that occurred as a result of the testing experience, the children's increased maturity, and other potentially influential factors.

An analysis of variance employing a repeated measures design demonstrates that the children in the Experimental school showed a greater increase in knowledge than the Control school. The differences were most impressive in the measures of knowledge and understanding of special effects, commercials, and advertising ($F=120.72$, p .0001). The items included in this analysis are: "(1) how does television make characters disappear?; (2) what advertising techniques are used to enhance products?; (3) what would you do if you liked a product that you saw advertised on television?; (4) who pays for television programs?; and (5) where should one write a letter regarding an unfair program or commercial?"

The children in the Experimental school also learned more lesson related vocabulary words than the children in the Control school ($F=23.85$, p .0001) (see Figure 2). The multiple-choice test consisted of ten vocabulary words, including *video, fiction, animation, sponsor,* and *prejudice.* Similarly, the children in the Experimental school improved more in their ability to identify videotaped examples of camera effects and special effects ($F=8.05$, p .005) (See Figure 3). The six effects included close-up shots, cuts, dissolves, edits, slow motions, and zoom shots.

Additional repeated measures analysis of variance were employed to determine whether the children retained the information that they had learned from the eight lessons. The follow-up test took place in February

1979. The analysis demonstrated that the children remembered the vocabulary words, effects and special effects, and advertising information that they had learned. The children in the Control school (School B) also tended to improve as a result of the repeated testing and/or maturation; however, between October and February the children in School A improved significantly more than the children in School B in terms of identifying effects and special effects and understanding commercials (p .001). These results are presented in Figure 1 and Figure 3. Since the children in both schools improved significantly on the vocabulary test, these differences between the two samples are no longer significant (p =.15).

The February/March comparisons indicate that the second experimental group (School B) learned even more than the first experimental group (School A) had learned in the autumn phase of the study. There was a dramatic increase in knowledge and understanding of special effects, commercials, and advertising (F =200.00, p .0001) (see Figure 1). The children also learned lesson-related vocabulary (F =24.14, p .0001) (see Figure 2), and were able to identify new videotaped examples of camera effects and special effects (F =109.39, p .0001).

In order to determine whether or not the children could extend the knowledge gained in the classroom to another situation, they were tested on new material relating to a situation to which they had not been exposed before, but which involved the general area of special effects that they had studied. Results demonstrate that they were able to generalize their newly acquired information to this new situation (F =14.05, p .0005).

In addition, test results indicated that children in both schools were equally able to distinguish between real people, realistic characters, and fantasy characters. In both schools, however, there was some confusion between real people and realistic characters; for example, Mary Tyler Moore, the actress, was confused with "Mary Richards", the television producer whom she portrays in the show. The overwhelming majority of the children in both schools, however, knew that Wonder Woman is not a real person, and that the violence on television programs is not real.

DISCUSSION

Children's television viewing ranged between 1 and 40 hours per week; the mean was 15 hours, which is considerably below the national average of 20-30 hours for this age group. Parents' viewing averaged 10.5 hours each per week. There was a consistent relationship between parents' and children's viewing. A stepwise multiple regression evaluated the extent to which sex; grade; age; IQ; birth order; number of siblings, a parentally imposed limit on television viewing; and parents' educational levels, weekly television viewing time, and time spent watching violent television programs predicted the amount of time the child spends watching television each week. Heavy viewers tended to be male, to have parents who watch alot of television, and to have no parentally imposed limit on television viewing. These four variables accounted for 34 per cent of the variance (F=21.21, p .0001). The relationship between sex and children's viewing was apparently related to the fact that two of the four television viewing weeks were during the end of the baseball season, and the boys were more likely to watch televised baseball games than were the girls. For the two viewing weeks in November (after baseball season was over), sex was unrelated to the amount of television viewing.

The amount of time that the children spent watching action/violent television programs was predicted by their watching more television, male sex, older age, and fathers watching more action/violent programs and fewer other programs. When the amount of the child's total viewing time was controlled, the other four variables accounted for 27 per cent of the variance for viewing action/violent programs.

A research staff member was present during most of the lessons in each classroom and was able to record what transpired. In addition, teachers met with the research staff for a feedback session at the end of the study in both schools. Thus we were able to evaluate exactly what occurred during the actual lessons. Teachers were well prepared and enthusiastic about the lessons. They tended to follow the lesson plans and make some minor modifications to fit classroom needs and interests. In general, children were attentive to most of the lesson content, and especially enjoyed recognizing many of their favorite TV programs on the videotapes.

Certain parts of the lessons were particularly interesting to the children, such as the special effects used for disappearing, bionic jumps and slow motion. We were able to bring videotape equipment into the classroom, and helped the children make a tape of each other "disappearing" which was played back for them. In addition, some of the children wrote and performed their own commercials which were also taped. Not only were the mechanics of television exciting to the children, but lively discussions took place dealing with topics such as stereotypes, aggression and commercials. For example, when one third grade teacher asked which characters on TV they liked, many boys said the Hulk. When questioned about this preference, they replied, "he's big", "strong", "powerful", "He can do anything." But when she asked if the Hulk was "happy", the class responded with such answers as "No, he has a demon inside of him", "It's not good to be out of control", "He never knows when he'll be a different person."

The children had many comments to make about watching violent programs. One child said, he "didn't feel good," when he watched "violence." Several children said that they imitated characters on *CHiPS* or *Baretta* and that led to trouble in the house. One child commented that violent programs are "put on the air so advertisers want you to keep watching so you'll buy what they show." Another said, "people learn from action shows not to do certain things." The children had watched such action shows as *Starsky & Hutch, CHiPS, The Incredible Hulk* and *Charlie's Angels.*

Many of the children also commented about toys they bought that were advertised on TV, and how "different" they looked when they actually got them at home. Differentiating among the four kinds of commercials was somewhat difficult for some of the children, but they seemed to grasp the techniques used to make products appear attractive such as lighting, music and endorsements. The lessons on special effects were extremely well-received. Despite an initial concern about our unveiling the mystery of TV, the children now understood the camera techniques and feel that they "were in on the secrets of TV." The children particularly enjoyed the animation segment, but had some difficulty understanding the techniques of chroma-key. This was not adequately explained on our tapes.

One of the most difficult concepts for the younger children was to understand the definition of personality trait. They could name superficial reasons for liking characters, but it was more difficult for them to define personality in terms of underlying characteristics. Although initially, some children were confused about the meaning of stereotypes, most were able to understand the concepts through the many concrete TV examples used and through their own examples from life experiences.

Finally, in the last lesson, where the emphasis was on the child's ability to "be in charge" of his TV viewing, the children gave many suggestions concerning TV. For example, some of the programs they did not want were "religious shows—they're too boring", "Adam-12, because it's too violent",: "bad commercials like "Bedding Barn" and "Crazy Eddy." The children felt keenly about writing to complain or praise a show to the following: "the company that puts on a show", the "director", the "sponsor", the "president of NBC", the "Federal Government." Some suggested "marching to the TV station" or "boycotting a station", or "calling the station manager." There obviously were strong sentiments expressed concerning a need to be heard.

CONCLUSIONS

The major finding of the study is that the materials developed were effective in teaching children about television production and techniques, and were also useful as a means of teaching vocabulary words, writing skills, mathematics, and critical thinking skills. Although these middle-class third, fourth, and fifth graders initially understood that television programs and commercials distort reality, the lessons were effective in teaching them to understand how this is done. It is also important to note that the teachers found the materials easy to use, with the brief training they were given. This is especially impressive since most of the teachers were not knowledgeable about the information to be covered, and were relatively unfamiliar with most of the children's favorite television programs and characters.

While it was not possible at this point to assess our ultimate goal of creating more discriminating TV consumers, (this would mean continual follow-up studies) the level of classroom discussions suggested the considerable value of teachers' attention to the medium. Homework assignments, such as those in which children were asked to record the degree of violence they saw, to rewrite commercials, or to propose alternatives to aggressive solutions to conflicts on the screen, indicated that the lessons on TV were provoking some serious thought about this popular medium.

The second major finding of the study is that the parents were very influential role models for their children's television viewing and for their attitudes towards television. The information concerning the parents' television viewing patterns and interests indicates that these variables were important predictors of children's television viewing habits. In addition, the parents apparently influenced their children's perceptions of the importance of television. In the questionaires, the children were asked how they would feel if "television would disappear from this planet tomorrow", with instructions to choose between responses ranging from "very, very sad/very, very angry" to "I would feel happy." Most of the children expressed considerable anger or unhappiness in response to this question; the children whose responses showed less distress were those who were older, whose fathers watched less television, and whose mothers were less well educated. These three variables accounted for 11 per cent of the variance (p .001).

Clearly, the children's strong interest in television reflected their parents' viewing habits. The reluctance of most of the parents to participate in the TV workshops that were offered and their apparent lack of interest in the research results indicate that even these well-educated middle-class parents were not very concerned about the impact of television on their children's development. In fact, the parents seemed to think that television was a problem for *other* children, especially less privileged children, rather than their own offspring. However, our data indicate that television viewing tends to be more strongly related to the examples set by the parents, rather than to expected predictors such as parents' educational levels, mothers' employment status, or child's IQ.

If the television industry and the majority of parents continue to be unresponsive to research results concerning television's effects on children, educators may have to show leadership by implementing curricula to teach children to be critical of the programs and commercials that they are watching. Television is now so pervasive a feature of daily life and of the growing child's world that it must become a subject for the regular educational curriculum. Our study suggests that children can be taught useful knowledge about the medium in the regular school curriculum. Tying in children's natural interest in TV with exercises in reading, writing and critical thinking has much to offer for the educator.

References

1. Anderson, J.A., & Ploghoft, M.E. *Receivership skills: The television experience.* Paper presented at the meeting of the International Communications Association, Acapulco, Mexico, 1980.

2. Atkin, C.K. *The effects of television advertising on children. Second year experimental evidence.* Unpublished Final Report, Office of Child Development, Department of Communication, Michigan, State University, 1975.

3. Barry, T.E. The effect of a modified disclaimer on inner-city vs. suburban children. *Proceedings,* American Marketing Association, August 1978.

4. Belson, W.A. *Television and the adolescent boy.* Hampshire, England: Saxon House, 1978.

5. Busby, L.J. Sex-role research on the mass media. *Journal of Communications,* 1975, *25* (4), 107-131.

6. Collins, W.A. The developing child as a viewer. *Journal of Communications,* 1975, *25* (4), 35-44.

7. Collins, W.A. Temporal integration and children's understanding of social information on television. *American Journal of Orthopsychiatry,* 1978, *48,* 198-204.

8. Comstock, G., Chaffee, S., Katzman, N., McCombs, M., & Roberts, D. *Television and human behavior.* New York: Columbia University Press, 1978.

9. Eron, L.D. *Sex, aggression, and fantasy.* Paper presented at the meeting of the Midwestern Psychological Association, Chicago, May 1979.

10. Galst, J.P., & White, M.A. The unhealthy persuader: The reinforcing valve of television and children's purchase-influencing attempts at the supermarket. *Child Development,* 1976, *47,* 1089-1096.

11. Gerbner, G. Cultural indicators: The case of violence in television drama. The *Annals* of the American Academy of Political and Social Science, March, 1970.

12. Hinton, J.L., Seggar, J.F., Northcott, H.C., & Fontes, B.F. Tokenism and improving imagery of blacks in TV drama and comedy. *Journal of Broadcasting,* 1973, *18,* 423-432.

13. Lefkowitz, M.M., Eron, L.D., Walder, L.O., & Huesmann, L.R. *Growing up to be violent.* Elmsford, N.Y.: Pergamon Press, 1977.

14. Liebert, D.E., Sprafkin, J.N., Liebert, R.M., & Rubinstein, E.A. Effects of television commercial disclaimers on the product expectations of children. *Journal of Communication,* 1977, *27,* 118-124.

15 Robertson, T.S., & Rossiter, J.R. Children and commercial persuasion: An attribution theory analysis. *Journal of Consumer Research,* 1974, *1,* 13-20.

16. Singer, J.L., & Singer, D.G. *Television-viewing and imaginative play in preschoolers: A developmental and parent-intervention study.* Unpublished Progress Report (#2), Yale University, 1978.

17. Singer, J.L., & Singer, D.G. *Television-viewing and imaginative play in preschoolers: A developmental and parent-intervention study.* Unpublished Progress Report (#4), Yale University, 1979.

18. *The spider's web.* Boston: WGBH Radio, 1979.

19. Sternglanz, S., & Serbin, L. Sex role stereotyping on children's television programs. *Developmental Psychology,* 1974, *10,* 710-715.

20. Surgeon General's Scientific Advisory Committee on Television and Social Behavior. *Television and growing up: The impact of televised violence.* Washington, D.C.: Government Printing Office, 1972.

21. *Teaching with newspaper: A newsletter for undergraduate method instructors.* Washington, D.C.: American newspaper Publishers Association Foundation, 1978.

22. *Television awareness training.* New York: Media Action Research Center, 1979.

23. Ward, S., Wackman, D.B., & Wartella, E. *Children learning to buy: The development of consumer information processing skills.* Beverly Hills, Calif.: Sage, 1976.

24. *The way we see it: A program to improve critical televiewing skills.* Idaho: State Department of Education, 1978.

SECTION III

Critical Viewing Skills Projects for the Secondary Level

Critical viewing curricula are faced with substantially different problems and concerns at the secondary level from the elementary grades. Much of the concern of exploitation of the child audience and overuse of television by that audience is missing. Persons of high school age show sharp declines in television use; peer pressure is more of a problem than overcommercialization.

The New York and Oregon, district-wide television based curricula which were reported here represented two of the longest running, continuous efforts in critical viewing skills. Both districts reported that the successful adoption of CRS curricula was dependent on teacher, administrator and parent commitment plus the flexibility of design which permit diverse classroom adoption.

Two of the four projects funded by the Office of Education also were reported in this section. (All four project directors spoke to the conference.) Both reports provided the goals and basic approaches used by the projects.

A&R discussion groups underlined the shift at the secondary level from thereapeutic issues to concerns about the increasing role of the high school student in society. One group reported: From both a personal and social development perspective, a democratic society requires that its members be able to obtain the best data available, analyze and evaluate it and then carry through with the appropriate action. Therefore, given the magnitude of the media as an informational source, it is in the best interests of ourselves as individuals, and as members of a democratic society, to promote the development of these skills."

Television Receivership Skills Program in the East Syracuse - Minoa Central Schools

Suzanne Schaff

INTRODUCTION

East Syracuse - Minoa's project in Television Viewing Skills has proceeded in four phases during the past four summers. Each summer since 1976 interested teachers in Social Studies and Language Arts grades 6-12 have come together for five half-days of orientation and curriculum planning. Dr. Milton Ploghoft has served as a consultant during each phase.

Suzanne Schaff is a teacher in the East Syracuse Minor Central School System.

HISTORY

1976: Teachers were introduced to the concept of teaching T.V. viewing skills to students and became familiar with some of the materials developed by Dr. Ploghoft and Dr. James Anderson. This group concentrated on discussing ways to help students be more critical viewers of T.V. commercials.

1977: New members were added to the group, but still participants were either Social Studies or Language Arts teachers in grades 6-12. After reviewing the concept of teaching T.V. Viewing Skills, this group made the decision that T.V. Viewing Skills would be a part of the existing curricula in Social Studies and Language Arts. Teachers wrote objectives for their subjects and grade levels. The product at the end of this workshop was a compilation of some objectives for teaching T.V. Viewing Skills where they naturally fit within existing curricula of the teachers represented. For instance: Sixth grade Language Arts teachers wrote objectives for critical viewing of T.V. commercials within their unit *The Language of Symbols*. Tenth grade Language Arts teachers wrote objectives to apply to skills taught in the unit *Semantics* to the television presentation of news, drama and entertainment. Social Studies teachers wrote objectives for critical viewing of T.V. news which fit a number of existing units at different levels. Sociology teachers wrote objectives to ask students to apply skills and understandings of survey methods to their own television viewing habits. In some cases the same objectives were written for a junior high level subject and again for a high school level so that students at higher levels would be approaching the same objective on a more sophisticated level.

1978: The first part of this workshop was devoted to an overview of other projects on T.V. Critical Viewing Skills and discussion of where we were and where we needed to go. We then broke into groups of social studies teachers and groups of language arts teachers to begin to write actual exercises to realize the objectives we had written the summer before. At the end of this workshop we had developed some exercises to meet some of the objectives. We concentrated on applying onjectives to entertainment programming.

1979: The first week of this workshop was designed to meet some of the expressed needs of the entire group. In addition, individuals wrote curriculum proposals to develop materials to meet the objectives of their particular subject area and grade level. The group expressed a need to know in some detail what other projects were doing so we could have some sense of our own. Lynne Brenner, Ganek, a writer of instructional materials for the WNET - T.V. project spent a day discussing the "Critikit" package with us. There was also a need to understand the actual workings of television stations and television production. To meet these needs, we spent one day at a local commercial station, another at the local public T.V. station. We also arranged for a two day crash course in T.V. production techniques at a local college. Thus, the group workshop for this summer was mainly experimental. Beyond this, individuals developed mor specific objectives and activities for the critical viewing of T.V. news and commercials. A high school group used the summer's experiences to begin a unit on T.V. production.

NEEDS

This curriculum project spans seven grade levels in two different subject areas. The teachers represented are housed in at least four different buildings. The need for a leader or coordinator is obvious.

There is a need for the program to be more formally defined and implemented. If the program is to remain exclusively within the social studies and language arts there is a need to familiarize more teachers in these areas with the program or to more specifically define the grade levels and subject areas where the Viewing Skills Program will be implemented.

If the program is to be expanded to other subject areas, how will this be accomplished?

The actual classroom use of the materials needs to be encouraged, increased and evaluated.

Equipment needs were met in the past. We have sought to make video-tape equipment more available this year. We also need more training in the use of this equipment.

We need more clarity on the legal use of T.V. taps for classroom teaching.

Above all we need to become a working, interacting group throughout the year to fully realize the implementation of the T.V. Viewer Skills Program in the classroom.

SUMMARY

This project has developed slowly but steadily over the past four summers. The progression has been logical and we have now reached a stage where our own goals have become more clear and comfortable. We have been a small, closed group who really only shared a summer romance. The time has come to make some decisions as to how to formally implement this program, how to open the project to others, how to insure ongoing dialogue and participation. Central to all these felt needs is the need for a leader with the commitment, the time and the power to make this a reality.

Television Viewer Skills Project
Eugene, Oregon School District

By Melva Ellingsen

INTRODUCTION

The Television Viewer Skills Project developed by Drs. Ploghoft and Anderson has been used in the Eugene School District in a number of ways since it was initially piloted in its original form in 1970. It has been taught to students at the upper elementary level, the junior high level and in the high schools. Its presentation and inclusion in curriculum has been in the form of a choice curriculum at the elementary level, as an elective course at the secondary level, as a part of a language arts program, a social studies program in both elementary and secondary schools and in conjunction with the broadcasting programs taught in the high schools. An example of an elective secondary offering as taught is "Speech and Television Viewing." It continues to be taught in a variety of ways and appears to have become a permanent part of the curriculum in the Eugene School District. The project received greatest emphasis when it was used by an alternative school as a framework for the general curriculum.

Melva Ellingsen is a curriculum specialist for School District 4J, Eugene Public Schools, Eugene, Oregon.

THE INTEGRATION OF RECEIVERSHIP SKILLS WITH ON-GOING PROGRAM

Determination of the structure or context within which Television Viewer Skills have been and are being taught is based upon the goals of the curriculum, both in content and skills. For example, the study of news and documentaries, the development of observation skills, identification of persuasion techniques and influence upon the consumer are likely to appear in social studies; the analysis of acting and dramatic forms in entertainment programs, commercials and news (particularly weather) fall within the performing arts; speech, delivery, and script writing are taught as language arts. The program provides an excellent basis and framework for an integrated curriculum in addition to establishing techniques for reaching the major goal, the teaching of critical viewing skills.

INSERVICE SUPPORT REQUIRED

Inservice during the school year and summer workshops have been essential to the success of the viewer skills instructional program. Inservice provides staff training with program content and use of video equipment necessary to the project. The inservice dealing with content is important for understanding the goals and how the content is designed to achieve these goals. It is equally important that the teacher become familiar and comfortable with the video equipment. It is interesting to note that in many cases the students are much more knowledgeable about and eager to work with the equipment when the instructor is fearful of and reluctant to use electronics equipment to its full potential. Inservice is also essential as a motivational factor. New information and the sharing of experiences is an important key to the success of the program. In my opinion and experience, inservice is the only force which will make the program go; administrative mandate may initiate its use but it will not provide the support to sustain it.

Summer workshops have provided the opportunity in Eugene for program modification to meet community and school needs and to develop additional activities for use with the project. An example of program modification may be seen in the news component. Workshop participants developed activities which provided a relationship between national news, state and regional news, and local news in the context of media sources available in the immediate community. Students in turn gather news and create their own content and delivery over a student video medium to the school. Other activities include retrieval charts, modified diaries, parent communiques, and performance ideas. These workshops have also been motivational and important in planning an inservice plan for the coming school year.

PROGRAM SUCCESS—CONTENT

The commercial segment of the program has been particularly successful since it has special appeal to students. In addition to their interest in being able to observe persuasion techniques they experience real success in learning how to manipulate an audience, thus demonstrating conceptualization of critical viewing skills. The success experience, as teachers recognize, is a definite plus for the student—his/her self-concept improves, the socialization process with classmates becomes more positive, and the student's, seemingly inherent, love for acting can be motivational to improvement in other areas of the curriculum. Student registration shows that those who have this program in the elementary schools often elect a class at the junior high or senior high level which contains components from the project.

PROGRAM SUCCESS—COMMUNITY

Critical viewing instruction has created a very desirable link with the Eugene community—the parents, community college and media systems, radio, television and newspaper. The program has had interest and support from the parents in several ways. They share the students' activities in keeping a diary of daily viewing and attest to the fact that they, the parents, also become more critical viewers of television as a result of this experience. They have contact with the schools through communiques used in the program. Project materials have been used with concerned parental groups who would like to influence program choices by the local stations. The community college has used the project materials in a manner similar to those of the high school broadcasting classes. The college instructor and the students have shown a great deal of interest in the school district program and practicum situations have resulted. The media have demonstrated the greatest interest—the newspaper has featured the project in full page coverage, television stations have included clips from the instruction in the 6 p.m. news broadcast, and radio stations have provided resources to the instructional staff.

THE CHALLENGE TO INNOVATION

The major challenge to the teacher of the Television Critical Viewing Skills Project, in addition to gaining mastery of the equipment, is the heavy demand of accountability to raise test scores, meet broad goals, and state minimum standards. It is difficult for the teacher to "add" curriculum in the day of "back-to-basics." An integrated program seems more desirable and has greater chance of success than an "add-on" and I strongly recommend this approach. While it is difficult to find time in the crowded school day to deal with a project such as the Television Viewer Skills in all probability these skills are more basic than the traditional three "R's." When one examines the research on viewer use in contrast to usage of reading, writing, and computation in life-long skills usage, evidence points to a greater need for viewer skills. Since television has become a major influential force in society, and it is the school's responsibility to provide the students with skills to survive in that society, instruction in the use and understanding of critical viewing is a must in a responsible curriculum.

The Critical Television Viewing Project For High School Students

By Donna Lloyd-Kolkin

INTRODUCTION

Americans spend a great deal of time watching television. On the average, they watch for over four hours each day, or about 25 per cent of their waking hours. For the average viewer that totals up to nine years in front of the set by the age of 65!

How well is this time used? Parents and high school teachers are now interested in this question as they see the impact television has on the lives of American youth. By the time they are 18, young viewers will have devoted more time to television than to teachers, yet few schools provide instruction to help their students evaluate television critically and make conscious decisions about its use.

Commercial television programming provides its own curriculum of values, lifestyles, and persuasive messages which can influence careless viewers more powerfully than it influences thoughtful, critical viewers. Teachers can encourage their students to be aware, and can equip them with the skills and information needed to view selectively and wisely.

Donna Lloyd-Kolkin is the project director of the Far West Laboratory for Educational Research's television high school curriculum development project. Materials are available from her at 1855 Falsom St. San Francisco, CA 94103.

Teaching Television Viewing Skills

Teachers are including critical television viewing skills in their lesson plans for a variety of reasons. This is an era in which educators are concerned with competency-based education. It is certainly true that a basic competency is the ability to make good use of the visual media pervasive in American life. Educators now define "literacy" as the ability to deal knowledgeably with all the communication media. They are giving students the same tools with which to relate to television as they are giving to relate to print media, literature, music, and art.

This is also an era of "back-to-basics" in the classroom. Teachers are discovering that they can capitalize on students' natural interest in television and use it as subject matter while teaching the basic skills of reading, writing, and critical thinking.

The topic of television is relevant to students' daily lives and it touches on many aspects of their learning, especially in the fields of English and Social Studies. No longer is television dismissed as a competitor to education; examination of television's art, industry, persuasive arguments, and effects is becoming an integral part of American education today.

CRITICAL TELEVISION VIEWING SKILLS FOR HIGH SCHOOL STUDENTS

In 1978, the U.S. Office of Education sponsored a conference with the Library of Congress entitled TELEVISION, THE BOOK, AND THE CLASSROOM to examine the role of television in the education of American children and youth. Educators, parents, librarians, and broadcasters attended the conference and voiced concern about television's influence. As a result of this concern, four curriculum development projects in critical television viewing skills were funded by the U.S. Office of Education, and they are currently creating materials geared toward elementary, middle school, high school, and post-secondary levels.

These critical television viewing skills projects have a nationwide scope and offer a complete program of classroom materials, family materials, and training workshops for parents and teachers. They join ranks with a variety of other programs aimed at utilizing television for teaching including TV script reading curriculum projects, teachers' guide to commercial television programs, and parent involvement workshops.

The high school project contracted by the U.S. Office of Education is located at Far West Laboratory for Educational Research and Development in San Francisco. They worked with Boston's public television station WGBH to develop a high school textbook, teacher's guide, and family guide about television. They also offer workshops for educators and parents nationwide to introduce these materials and demonstrate methods for teaching critical television viewing skills to youth. (For a review of the curricular activities, see Appendix A.)

WHAT ARE CRITICAL TELEVISION VIEWING SKILLS?

In developing the high school textbook about television, Far West Laboratory defined four major critical television viewing skills:

1. *Ability to evaluate and manage one's own television viewing behavior.*

Television can be misused if viewing becomes a substitute for other important activities. Critical viewers know their personal goals and decide when to watch television based on those goals. Many young children are unable to do this, so parents often set limits on their viewing hours. Teenagers, on the other hand, can be taught to assess their own viewing behavior, think about their goals, and make conscious decisions about their own best use of television.

2. *Ability to question the reality of television programs.*

Television programs may look realistic, but economic, technological, and production value decisions affect the creation and broadcast of any television show. Critical viewers know about the production techniques involved in staging, shooting, and editing a television program. They think about the television industry's goals and priorities. By evaluating the images and messages chosen by the industry, viewers understand that there are many factors which make television content different from reality.

3. *Ability to recognize the arguments employed on television and to counterargue.*

Commercials, political advertisements, and public service messages bombard viewers with persuasive arguments. Television programs are also persuasive because they carry repeated messages about values and life choices such as, "Violence solves problems," or "Youth and beauty are the pathways to success." Critical viewers analyze the validity of television arguments. They can identify persuasive techniques, point out fallacies and assumptions, and express their own values in relation to those presented on television.

4. *Ability to recognize the effects of television on one's own life.*

Television viewing can have an impact on leisure time, health, and productivity and television's messages can affect career aspirations, aggression and stereotyping, to name a few. American society is populated by television viewers who are shaping the world every day. Consequently, everyone, viewer and non-viewer alike, is affected by television. By recognizing the effects of television on their lives, viewers use television for their own needs and are not "used" by it. Critical users view selectively, judge television quality, and develop the skills to appreciate programs that offer the best in entertainment, information, instruction, and drama.

TEXTBOOK AND TEACHER'S GUIDE

The project at Far West Laboratory has developed a textbook and a teacher's guide. The high school textbook, entitled *Inside Television: A Guide to Critical Viewing,* focuses on the students' relationship to television

to help them make their own decisions about its use. The main text provides information about broadcasting and production, and covers:
* individual and national viewing habits
* the television industry; its history, economics, and regulations
* television's dramatic form and production techniques
* advertising and persuasive messages
* news and informational programming
* television content and its effects on viewers
* new developments in television technology and delivery

In addition to the expository text, students are given dozens of individual and group activities such as research projects, field visits, debate topics, personal TV viewing logs, and discussion questions, all structured to help them form their own opinions about television and develop analytical skills. For example, in one activity students look at the editing and camera techniques used in two TV commercials and explain how these techniques help enhance the mood and message of each commercial. In another activity, students examine the advantages and disadvantages of television by writing an assay to describe what their lives would be like without any television at all.

Students also use primary learning materials in the textbook such as television scripts, interviews with television professionals, and television industry documents to gain a first-hand view of the factors that go into television production and broadcast.

This combination of factual information, exploratory activities, and primary reading material provides students with a variety of approaches in understanding television. The accompanying teacher's guide offers daily lesson plans which can be used in a one-semester course about television or can be divided into seven smaller units for use in Social Studies, Media, and Language Arts classes. The textbook and teacher's guide use a wide range of resources and activities to encourage students to take greater responsibility for determining their own cultural environment.

THE FAMILY GUIDE TO TELEVISION

To extend critical viewing skills to the home environment the project has developed a guide for families. This collection of questions, quizzes, and games is designed to stimulate family discussion about television use at home. Does TV bring your family together or does it help everyone avoid each other? How does your family select programs to watch? How many hours per day do you spend watching TV and what are your reasons for watching?

American families have the television set on for an average of six-and-one-half hours each day. The *Family Guide to Television* can be a useful tool in helping families take a closer look at their relationship with this important "member of the family." It is available for free and will be distributed by the Consumer Information Center, Pueblo, Colorado 81009, beginning in January, 1980.

CRITICAL TELEVISION VIEWING SKILLS WORKSHOPS

As a fourth activity, the Critical Television Viewing Skills Project for High School Students offers workshops throughout the nation for parents and educators to help them teach critical viewing skills effectively. The workshops:
* describe the impact of television on American youth
* define critical television viewing skills
* provide teaching ideas
* introduce a variety of curriculum materials

The workshops cover the concepts and methodology fundamental for teaching this subject, and provide time for participants to share their ideas and concerns in small group activities. Participants receive curriculum materials and are placed on a mailing list to receive additional information about critical television viewing skills and the latest developments at Far West Laboratory.

Appendix A
Critical Television Viewing Skills Curriculum Outline
A Course For High School Students

Unit I, You and Television

This unit introduces students to television as a unique medium with a special role in the lives of people. Important to this unit is the students' logging of their own television viewing behavior, with opportunity to compare their viewing to several national averages.

Students will determine their own criteria by which to evaluate viewing patterns, taking into consideration television's characteristics and its influence on values and life styles. This will serve to introduce students to the themes that will be covered in depth throughout the curriculum.

Unit 2, The Television Industry

Unit 2 maps out the course of television and its organization including the networks, local stations, public television, the Federal Communications Commission, the role of the advertiser, the importance of ratings, and tactics of scheduling. Basic federal regulations regarding television are introduced so that students will comprehend the freedoms and constraints that are imposed on the industry.

Television distribution is examined as a business which, from the start, was automatically considered part of the American free enterprise system. The financing of programs and the relationships between producers, networks, and affiliates are examined. In light of the power and profitability of the medium, the fierce competition for high ratings and control of the airwaves is documented.

The development of television technology is described, showing its emergence as an invention of no parallel, embodying unique processes and effects. Future technologies and the debates regarding their regulation are also discussed.

Unit 3, Programs and Production

This unit enables students to analyze dramatic television programs in much the same way they might approach a novel or short story. Dramatic elements such as plot construction, characterization, dialogue, and pacing are discussed along with the constraints on dramatic form imposed by the nature of the television medium.

Following this analysis, the unit next considers how the elements of television production influence the nature of the programs on the air. Content covered includes television production choices (video vs. film, types of camera shots and lighting, music track, etc.), economic constraints on production, types of persons employed, and the teamwork required to put a program together to get it on the air. The outcome of this part should be a greater understanding that all TV programs are deliberately "staged" for technological and economic reasons. Students will also develop an appreciation of the singular aesthetic principles of television.

Unit 4, Selling

Selling, or advocacy programming, includes any television messages intended to persuade, such as commercials and political advertising. In Unit 4, students will learn to identify persuasive arguments and develop ways to counterargue. They will also be introduced to the impact of television on politics including voting behavior, political advertising, "image" politics, and ways in which political campaigns have changed.

In addition, this unit covers topics such as market research, the use of stereotypes in commercials, subliminal messages used to attract buyers, the size of advertising budgets, and the restrictions imposed by the Federal Trade Commission. The biases of advertising are discussed to point out that specific production techniques are chosen to suit specific goals and needs.

Unit 5, That's The Way It Is?

Unit 5 focuses on news and informational programming; their production techniques, their power to influence opinion, and the legal and social responsibilities of their creators.

The constraints on television coverage of the news are examined including time limitations, technological shortcomings, and news policies imposed by the networks.

The power of news programming is also discussed. Editorial decisions such as choice of stories, their order of presentation, the length of time devoted to them, and the selection of accompanying images all serve to influence the implicit messages of newscasts and make objective reporting a difficult and often impossible task. Elements of television news are contrasted with print news, and varieties of documentary programming are described.

Students will learn about the Fairness Doctrine and discuss the First Amendment rights of broadcasters. Interviews with newscasters are included covering a wide range of controversial issues.

Unit 6, The Television Environment

This unit has a dual focus: the nature of television content, and studies that have shown the effects of that content on viewers.

In the first part, students consider how television images compare to the real world. Portrayals of women, minorities, different age groups, and acts of violence are shown to be different from their real world counter-parts. Attention is given to stereotypes and to the social and personal values of the TV environment: for example, that violence resolves conflict, that good always subdues evil, that youth and beauty are the pathways to happiness and success, to name a few.

In the second part, research is cited which suggests that heavy television viewing has a significant effect on how people regard the real world. In confronting this issue, students conduct their own research and evaluate a question that is pivotal to this curriculum: To what degree should television reflect life's realities?

Unit 7, A Saving Radiance?

This unit is a re-cap of the entire curriculum and gives students the opportunity to reinforce and review the skills developed. It also presents a summary of new television technologies which are destined (by the mid-1980's) to erode the centralized programming power of the three commercial networks. While studying these new developments, students address the issue of regulating television in the lives of their children in years to come.

Section IV

Network and Association Activities

Educational responses are by no means limited to the activities that are undertaken by individual school districts, university developers, and federally supported projects. In the articles that follow here, the interests and efforts of two major networks and two national associations are presented. Following the presentations of the N.E.A. representative, the P.T.A. speaker and the ABC and NBC spokesperson, a conference participant lamented the lack of comparable concern and cooperation by parents, schools, and the television industry at the grass roots level.

Educational Projects At ABC Television
Pamela Warford

INTRODUCTION

In order to further expand television's public service commitment, the office of Community Relations was instituted with the ABC Public Relations Department in 1977. One of the major responsibilities of this department is to increase communication and understanding among broadcasters, educators, and parents. By providing educational materials for classroom use, by encouraging research efforts, and by expanding the opportunities for public dialogue, Community Relations is working to emphasize that the television medium can be useful and productive in helping educate children.

The integration of quality television programs into English and social studies curricula, the teaching of critical viewing skills, and the use of television scripts in reading programs are all evidence of a growing appreciation on the part of teachers toward the positive uses of television in the classroom. In order to facilitate formal and informal learning for educators, students, and parents, the following projects have been designed and implemented by ABC:

Pamela Warford is Director, Community Relations at the American Broadcasting Company. Copies of materials are available from her at 1330 Avenue of Americas, N.Y., N.Y. 10019.

Teachers' Guides

Teachers' guides help educators use quality programs in the classroom by providing background materials. Typically, a teachers' guide includes background information, a synopsis, and suggestions for activities tied in to a particular program. Through classroom discussion, these suggested activities help students understand concepts covered in the program, master knowledge, and develop skills. Study guides, as they are also known, additionally include a section on learning resources that lists related forms and a bibliography.

In past seasons, study guides have been developed for such ABC PROGRAMS AS *Roll of Thunder, Hear My Cry, Eleanor and Franklin,* and the rebroadcast of *Roots.* In 1979, Community Relations project included educational materials associated with *Friendly Fire,* and the Fall and Winter seasons of *ABC Afterschool Specials* and *ABC Weekend Specials.* Additionally, a viewers' guide to two television dramas on aging—*Valentine* and a special episode of *Family*—was prepared by the Cultural Information Service for use in adult education classes and inter-faith discussion groups. Most recently, Community Relations sponsored a similar guide to ABC's presentation of *Amber Waves.*

In early 1979, in conjunction with *Roots: The Next Generations,* ABC produced its most ambitious effort to date in the area of educational tie-ins. Three educational guides were developed and sponsored by ABC. The NAACP, the Anti-Defamation League of B'nai B'rith, and the National Council for the Social Studies, jointly produced a 16-page newspaper supplement entitled *The Record: The Black Experience in America, 1619-1979.* For use in interfaith group discussions, the National Council of Churches distributed 100,000 guides on the series to Catholic, Protestant, and Jewish religious educators. However, the backbone of our educational effort was the 16-page full color guide produced by the Chicago-based organization, Prime Time School Television. Over 200,000 copies were printed and distributed to educators nationwide. As a result of a National Education Association alert on the availability of this guide, Prime Time School Television received 200 to 300 requests a day from educators over a six-week period.

Another major component of the *Roots II* program for educators was developed because of the belief that the script to a television production is a valuable and appealing way to teach reading and writing. Through ABC's initiation, the Associated Press agreed to an unprecedented distribution of scripts of the first two-hour program to newspapers throughout the country.

ABC's of Children's Television: A progress Report.

In september, 1979, an informative guide describing the positive evolution of children's programming on the ABC Television Network was released. Entitled "The ABC's of Children's Television: A Progress Report," this guide reflects ABC's efforts to meet the entertainment and educational needs of today's young viewers.

"The ABC's of Children's Television" was sent to all ABC Television Network affiliates for use in their educational communities, and to over 3,500 elementary and secondary school librarians, teachers, education editors, and government officials.

Making the News

Making the News, a self-contained course on television news designed for high school students and teachers was distributed in October, 1979. This curriculum unit explores four major news formats: the evening news, the interview, the documentary, and the television magazine program.

Prepared by Prime Time School Television in cooperation with ABC news, the unit is designed as a 16-page lesson plan summarizing the different news formats and the relationship of each format to the critical decisions involved in news production—the selection of the issue or event, the structure of the story, the depth and length, and the perspective and objectivity maintained in the coverage.

Following the summary of each format are student viewing logs, suggestions for class projects and lesson ideas. Students are asked to examine the difficult decisions faced by television news producers and the broadcast industry as a whole.

Containing options for lessons spanning one month of classroom instruction, *Making the News* materials are adaptable to English, Social Studies, Journalism, or Media classes. While ABC News programs are used as models, students and teachers compare reporting among all three commercial networks and public television, as well as local newscasts and print journalism. This curriculum unit also proved to be of interest to college level instructors of media and journalism courses as well.

Research is being conducted by ABC to evaluate the effectiveness and appeal of this project with teachers and students. Preliminary results indicate that the majority of teachers surveyed were enthusiastic about student achievements and were interested in future use of the guide.

Watch the Program/Read the Book

A continuing ABC project involves the award-winning *ABC Afterschool Specials* and *ABC Weekend Specials.* In response to numerous requests from librarians for educational materials about programs based on books for children, ABC initiated in 1978 the monthly distribution during the school year of background materials on upcoming programs. These mailings are designed to encourage the reading and discussion of the particular book in conjunction with the program.

Distribution was set up with the cooperation of the American Library Association, which supplied a mailing list of more than 2,500 elementary and secondary school librarians across the country. With additional requests, the mailing list has grown to over 4,000. The background materials supplied to the librarians include: a display poster highlighting the scheduled specials that month; sceneries of each special; biographies of the authors; and bibliographies of additional works by the authors.

The response to this project has been gratifying. Approximately 1,500 letters from librarians and school officials expressing interest and appreciation for the project have been received since its inception.

The Yale Study

Television is different from other media forms; to use it properly, children must have the support and guidance comparable to that given in developing the skills and standards they apply to more traditional sources of information and entertainment. Critical viewing skills are designed to make children more aware of their video environment. One of the projects in this area is the 18-month study recently completed at Yale University and funded by an ABC grant.

The study (reported in Section II) tested an eight-week lesson course for use in the third, fourth, and fifth grades. Focusing on motivating children to use television in a more active manner, the study also shows ways in which parents and teachers can use the natural interest of children in television to enhance cognitive and social skills, including reading.

"Be A TV Reviewer"

Television can also be used to encourage children to write. This was exemplified by a pilot study ABC conducted entitled "Be A TV Reviewer." In this pilot study, teachers received posters and guidelines about what a TV reviewer does, and children were invited to send in reviews about any television program describing why they thought it was effective or not.

The pilot studies were conducted in White Plains, New York, and Sioux City, Iowa, with voluntary cooperation of the local superintendent and elementary school principals. Participation was open to children in grades two through six.

It was hoped, through this project, to encourage the child to think critically about programs watched, and then to write those thoughts.

Through a follow-up questionnaire sent to teachers who participated in the project, the network learned their reactions which were equally important. Several wrote that they had not previously utilized television to stimulate reading or writing in classrooms. Others wrote to say that this project suggested others, such as surveys of television viewing habits, polls of "best programs," and the creation of ideas for new shows.

The results showed that children can be discerning viewers. Several hundred reviews were received, and all indicated a high degree of motivation. ABC received typed reviews, art work accompanying the reviews, and program suggestions demonstrating creative imagination.

Here is a sample review on *The Love Boat:*

"I am writing about *The Love Boat* because I like the show the best. I like the program because the characters for the parts have a comical touch in what they say, except for those love parts. I can also relate to what they say and how they react in their situations.

I like the techniques of communicating by using humor and warmth. The program is about five friendly, understanding crew members. There are also guest star appearences on *The Love Boat.*

The people always have funny problems and are in love. I do not think that the dialogue is that realistic. However, you have to consider that this is a fantasy program."

Television is a reality in a child's world. We hope that teachers will use the medium as an audiovisual aid, along with ancillary materials to make television a valuable tool in the overall learning process.

National Education Association Activities in Receivership Skills Curricula

Karen Klass

INTRODUCTION

Teachers and parents are both expressing increasing degrees of reservation, annoyance and even anger at the impact television is having on the lives of their children. However, their bows to the inevitability of television's continued presence are not all negative. They are also investigating positive uses of the medium with more purpose.

To a great extent television has been admonished and heralded by the same prophets of doom and delight who greeted the discovery of the written language, moveable type, automobiles, radio and motion pictures—every invention which forced a change in lifestyle.

With television, perhaps, there is a significant distinction. Its impact is so pervasive that children spend more time in front of the set than inside the classroom, and most see more of the network performers than of their natural parents.

It's no wonder that many teachers and parents feel a threat to their peimacy as instructors and value setters. The wonder is that both have benignly neglected the medium for so long. There are

---

Karen Klass is Communications Specialist for the National Education Association, Washington, D.C.

recent signs that the neglect is coming to an end at home and in the school.

I have just quoted the introductory paragraph in a three part series published last spring in the *Virginia Journal of Education;* a publication of an NEA affiliate, the Virginia Education Association. I think the attitudes expressed in the Journal, and the significance of the 5-7 pages in the three separate issues, points to a renaissance of thinking on the part of teachers - that TV can be a positive educational tool. The NEA has long been aware of the effect of mass media upon American youth. In 1969 our association passed a resolution calling for educators and parents to help children become intelligently critical viewers, listeners, and readers. For a number of years now, the NEA has conducted a special program of recommending certain radio and television shows to our 1.8 million members. The purpose of these recommendations is twofold: to encourage the scheduling of broadcasts with wide cultural, social, educational appeal; and, to advise teachers about meaningful programs in advance of broadcast; so that they may direct their students to more rewarding viewing.

We feel that this endeavor has helped to create a positive relationship between broadcasters and educators. With more viewers - sponsors and underwriters are increasing their participation in the production of more quality programs. One network reported in an informal survey, that an NEA endorsement was worth 2 rating points. That's 3 million homes, or 7 million viewers.

At the same time we are helping teachers with information about good radio and TV shows that can be useful instructional aids.

We are expanding our activities in this area by promoting projects such as the CBS Reading Program or NBC's parent workshops, which are designed by the broadcasters to help make their programs more educationally valuable. In the most recent secondary edition of the NEA magazine, *Today's Education;* ABC sponsored a 16 page insert prepared by Prime Time School TV which is a guide for use in English, Social Studies, and media classes, to teach students to analyze the content and influence of television news. The Feb/March issue of the elementary edition of *Today's Education* will carry a 4 page insert, again written by Prime Time, featuring material on the ABC "After School Specials."

One of the advantages of a large Association is the opportunity to promote activities of our local and state associations among the rest of the membership. I don't have the time to detail all of the TV projects which have been developed to date, but I will share with you some examples of interesting ways teachers have found to utilize TV.

In Virginia, two University of Richmond professors conducted a series of workshops last year and again this year, in which the television industry was examined from a humanist perspective. More than 30 industry creators and executives were brought to Virginia to participate. In New Jersey, teachers have been involved in a number of TV projects. Through the New Jersey Coalition for Better TV Viewing a coalition of parents, teachers, lawyers, and doctors, - members of the New Jersey Education Association have taken courses in TV literacy, participated in the FCC Children's TV Inquiry, and even lobbied for a much needed VHF station in their state. The delegate assembly of the Iowa State Education Association directed that association, last year, to work with other organizations in an effort to try and increase parent involvement in determining what, and how much television, is watched by youngsters. A campaign was developed in cooperation with the Iowa PTA, the Association of Iowa Educational Administrators, Iowa Medical Society, Inter-Church Media, the Iowa State University, and the Iowa Contact for Action for Children's Television.

The project included an activity guide for parents to plan a weekly non-school TV schedule, a 1/2 hour panel discussion on TV viewing taped by a Des Moines TV station, and distributed around the state, a 30 second PSA produced by a Des Moines ad agency on the importance of parent involvement in children's viewing habits; plus seminars for teachers on TV and values which were held in conjunction with the ISEA mobile inservice training job program, including a resource kit of instructional materials. Bill Sherman, our Iowa Communications Director, is here and available for more details.

In Southern California last year, the NEA held a training workshop for a number of Orange County and L.A. County teachers. The purpose of this workshop was to acquaint teachers with available materials to argument the use of TV in the classroom - and to help teachers become better evaluators of the television programs themselves. As a result of this experience the NEA has recommended several teachers to west coast TV producers who were seeking some assistance in developing scripts that would be appropriate and useful for children.

Many of our state associations have used their monthly magazines, as in the case of Virginia, to help their members use television. Last October the *Pennsylvania School Journal* chose to reprint an NEA piece on propaganda techniques in its article on "Ways to Use TV in your Teaching." One of the 13 methods discussed suggested that students write TV scripts for commercials, purposely using techniques such as bandwagon, card stacking, escape and fantasy, testimonial, transfer, etc. to teach the powerful affect of certain kinds of language. The *Ohio Schools* magazine, in April of this year, included an article on 30 ways to use TV. The story mentioned an excellent film, "Seeing Through Commercials" - which teaches children to understand TV ads - the Ohio Education Association keeps the film available, with the study guide, for member teachers to use.

Last month, the Vermont Education Association borrowed segments from Ohio and Virginia, and published 28 curriculum ideas in their monthly newspaper.

One of the first examples of teachers using television can be found in Baltimore County Maryland. "Project TV Awareness" was conceived by an elementary teacher who received and NEA fellowship to develop a "television literacy" curriculum. The project involved the participation of the PTA Council and the Board of Education in Baltimore County. The program was piloted in 4 elementary schools, and included educational programs for children and parents, in-school activities, parent related activities, and school-related activities. A further project tapped the resources and funds from the Teachers Association of Baltimore County, and two Baltimore TV stations, which produced a parent guide of family activities to develop television literacy. The complete details of this innovative project, which has now been integrated into the curriculum of *all* Baltimore County elementary schools, can be obtained from Camille Faith, the teacher who created it, who is here representing the Maryland State Teachers Association. Before I conclude my remarks, I do want to mention two activities involving television in which the NEA has been very involved. The first, is the FCC Children's TV Inquiry conducted by the FCC task Force on children's TV, and whose report was just released last Tuesday. Last year our members participated in the consumer workshops which were held around the country to discuss the issue. And, with the help of many interested and informed teachers, we filed comments to the Inquiry. We are anxiously following the activities of the Commission regarding any action they may take. Secondly, we were and are, very active in watching the legislation regarding the re-write of the Federal Communications Act of 1934, specifically where it relates to broadcasting. Our national convention passed a resolution calling for a strong effort towards maintaining the "public interest" in the act, and we will continue to work toward that end.

In conclusion, I'd like to reference the title of this conference "Children and Television - Implications for Education" by briefly commenting on the most recent issue of Phi Delta Kappan magazine. It features a number of articles on TV, one: "Video Valhalla and Open Education" by Charles Whaley and George Antonelli of the University of North Carolina, I found particularly interesting. Their piece, peppered with advertising jargon, compared Dick Clark's "American Bandstand" with open education. In their opinion, Dick Clark, as a "perfect non-directive teacher/host," provides the same self-indulgent narcissistic environment as an open classroom.
Whaley and Antonelli feel that we are "moving from the school of hard knocks to the school with soft spaces." I think they have missed the point. As educators, our overall concern should not be about the hit tunes or pimple creams, any more than it should be with different teaching styles. But what is important is the ability of our children to learn.

In another Kappan article, Neil Postman of NY University reflects that the "real progamatic issue, is not TV, but its relationship to other systematic teachings in the information environment. The question is, to what extent can the biases of TV be balanced by the biases of other information systems, particularly the school?" Postman defines TV and school as curricula. Stating that "curriculum is a specifically constructed information system whose purpose, in its totality, is to influence, teach, train, or cultivate the mind and character of youth." "Schools and TV," he say's, "are both total learning systems. With a special way of organizing time and space; their messages are encoded in special forms and moved at different rates of speed; each has its special way of defining knowledge, its special assumptions about the learning process, and its own special requirements concerning how one must attend to what is happening. Moreover, each has a characteristic subject matter, ambience, and style, all of which reflect the unique context within which one experiences what is going on."

So the challenge is there. If we accept TV as a positive teaching tool and presumably that's why we're here, we must be wary of its faults as well. The TV frame is a mirror of our society, and to quote NEA Executive Director Terry Herndon in the recent Journal of The Council on Children and Television, which he chairs: "even more than critical viewing skills, our children must be taught how to challenge, hypothesize, inquire, document, evaluate and make intelligent choices. They must be encouraged to create not just absorb."

The P.T.A. Critical Viewing Skills Project

Marion R. Young

INTRODUCTION

A six-year-old boy walked into a drugstore and asked the clerk for a box of Stayfree Minipads. When asked why he wanted the item, the boy explained that he was going horseback riding the next day, and a TV commercial he had seen showed a happy young woman galloping across the screen, announcing that she enjoyed horseback riding much more now that she used Stayfree Minipads.

This true story, while amusing, illustrates the very real persuasive powers of television and TV advertising. Some examples of this persuasive power are far from amusing. A child shoots his brother by accident, imitating a television airing of the movie DIRTY HARRY; a young girl is raped by a gang of youngsters using a beer bottle after the TV movie BORN INNOCENT shows a similar incident; a mentally retarded youth throws his baby sister out of the apartment window to her death because he is convinced she is the devil, trying to possess him—just like the baby he had seen earlier in a TV promotion for a coming movie.

The examples are numerous—and tragic. But they point out quite graphically what we have known for some time. Television does exert a

---

Marion R. Young is consultant to the National PTA TV Action Center in Chicago.

powerful influence on all of us—and on children particularly.

Today 98 percent of all Americans own at least one television set. Sixty-five percent get their complete diet of news and current events from TV, without ever reading a newspaper or magazine. Before graduating from high school, and American youth has viewed 18,000 hours of television programming; before even entering kindergarten, most youngsters have spent more hours in front of a TV than they would need to earn a college degree.

There is no doubt. Americans are watching record amounts of television. It is an easy way to obtain information, to relax and be entertained, to quiet the children so that they do not frazzle our nerves after a hard day or waken us too early on a Saturday morning. Television has become a mainstay in our lives—a miracle "drug" for any problem we might encounter. Boredom, lack of time or energy to read the daily news or to plan interesting family activities these problems are all solved with the flick of the TV's magic "on" switch.

Some of us remember the birth of television. We gathered in a darkened room to stare at a flickering blue image on a tiny screen. Friends and neighbors were invited for the special treat. Roller derby, wrestling, Super Circus—even the test pattern. It was a miracle!

But we haven't outgrown our awe of this electronic marvel. No one taught us to critically assess the new medium, yet suddenly we were responsible for evaluating programming—not only for ourselves, but for our children. Parents and teachers are finding themselves trapped in a Never-Never Land. The reality base of a relatively un-televisioned youth had enabled the majority of parents and teachers to subconsciously discard unworthy TV messages. Our children, who are and have been growing up in the shadow of the TV blitz, do not have the advantage of a non-electronic reality base. From the cradle, television has taken an important role in forming who and what our children will become.

Most of the available studies on the effects of television on children deal with violence and aggressive behavior. However, parents and teachers are reporting more and more that children's behavior patterns are being altered in more subtle ways.

We find our children unable to stick with a problem. They lack the attention span and patience to work at a project until it is completed. Armed with the instant learning experience of even such acclaimed programs as SESAME STREET, children are unwilling and unable to focus their attention on the relative boredom of the classroom teacher—Big Bird is much more fun.

A TV commercial shows a freckle-faced boy eating a bowl of "power-packed" breakfast cereal. Then he goes outside and hits a ball over the fence.

A TV father tells his son to mow the lawn; fifteen seconds later the lad is in the kitchen drinking lemonade—a perfectly manicured yard in the background the only evidence of his toil.

Nowhere do our children see the hours of practice and work that went into being able to perform the athletic feat, or the time and patience needed for the young boy to mow the lawn. All they see on any program or commercial is the result of these efforts.

On television, a major family crisis is solved in thirty or sixty minutes. Little problems take only seconds. Children and parents usually begin and end the program in perfect harmony and rapport with one another, with the problems and concerns of family life painlessly erased before the end-of-program theme song.

Youngsters who absorb television's constant message of instant gratification believe this is the way life should be. Anything else is "a hassle." They expect immediate relief from headache pain, and instant popularity if they use the right toothpaste, buy the right deodorant and wear the right clothes. With 18,000 hours of instant TV entertainment at the flip of a switch, it is no wonder that the instant gratification of drugs, alcohol and sex are so attractive to our youth. It is no wonder that our own family life appears weak and unappealing next to its TV counterpart.

We have been unwitting accomplices to this degeneration of our children's productivity and creativity. We innocently stood by and cheered when our three-year-old learned the alphabet from SESAME STREET. We chuckled when our teen-aged son was heard whistling "I'm a New Freedom Lady." Then we gasped when we heard of youngsters hurting and killing each other—imitating violent scenes from TV. "That child must be unbalanced. My child isn't affected that way," we reassured ourselves.

How long are we going to keep our eyes closed to the harmful effects of our convenient babysitter, and rationalize away a disintegration of our children's social behavior? The progress is gradual, but that does not lessen its devastating effect.

We didn't really push the issue when our children said they could do homework and watch television at the same time. More and more often, chores like cleaning their rooms or washing the dishes were put off "until after my program is over." When we visited friends and relatives the kids were bored, so they watched television. We vaguely realized that they weren't communicating much, but after all, adult conversation can be tedious for children, and the TV kept their interruptions to a minimum.

Our youngsters began high school and we couldn't wait for the excitement of football games and school activities to become part of our family life. But they didn't attend. "That's bogus," the kids said. "That stuff is for creeps and rah-rahs with nothing better to do." They called up a few friends and watched SATURDAY NIGHT LIVE.

But we didn't worry too much. At least they were at home instead of out running around, getting into trouble like so many youngsters today. We rationalized every step of our children's television-led withdrawal from family and from society.

With television now occupying so much of a child's time and providing so many artificial "experiences," it is up to us—parents, teachers, concerned viewers—to help children learn to evaluate television's messages. We must give them the tools and help them to use these tools in determining which programs and which messages are valuable and worthwhile to them.

After all, TV is not an evil invention to be shunned. At its best, television provides us with excellent entertainment and information. Jacques Cousteau, Shakespeare, movies, documentaries, high drama and enchanting comedy—even man's first steps on the moon. Television can and does bring us all of these things. But we must learn, and in learning, teach our children to watch television selectively.

Through its TV Action Center, the National PTA helps parents and teachers evaluate programs aired on television. The Center also helps parents learn how to exercise their influence in convincing the networks to improve the quality of the programs they present.

The best time to learn to evaluate television is during childhood - when attitudes and values are still being formed. That is why the National PTA's TV Action Center is now developing a curriculum designed to hone the viewing skills of children from kindergarten through the twelfth grade.

"Special Effects" was chosen as the first unit to be developed because of the immediate physical danger to children who attempt to copy stunts they see performed on television. By showing children *how* these feats are created, the curriculum unit will demonstrate not only the danger of imitating these feats without the necessary equipment and training but also will illustrate that on TV things aren't always what they appear to be.

Work on a Family Awareness Curriculum, paid for by funds from The Edna McConnell Clark Foundation in New York, will show students *how* and *why* TV families differ from real families.

One of the PTA's and the Clark Foundation's major concerns is children in non-traditional families. Adoptive children, foster children, single-parent families, and extended families receive short shrift, the Foundation feels, on too many TV schedules. Often children in these circumstances are frustrated by their inability to conform to the "happy family" standards set forth on programs aired by networks during prime-time hours.

By teaching these children to compare and contrast their own particular circumstances with the circumstances they observe on television, the Family Awareness Curriculum will help these youngsters recognize *how* TV families are *not* true to life. In the process, this curriculum should help these children gain an increased appreciation and acceptance of their own family units.

Another segment of the curriculum - called "Persuasive Techniques" - is still on the "drawing board," where it will remain till funds are found to bring it to life. Once produced, "Persuasive Techniques" will make students aware of production methods that are used to evoke a desired mood or attitude in viewers.

Dramatic lighting, music, camera angles, and careful editing are used by television to create a specific emotional response. In this new curriculum, once it is launched, both technical and artistic "persuaders" will be studied - including emotional language in scripts and the portrayal of certain roles.

Exploring the various aspects of television - from the technical through the artistic - will help children learn to discriminate between the fantasy and the reality of television programming.

By making children more aware of what they are viewing, the National PTA hopes to diminish the harmful impact of television on their attitudes and values, and to create a new generation of viewers who will seek out and demand programs of high quality.

What The TV Industry Is Doing To Help Youth

Jack Blessington

INTRODUCTION

This topic almost demands a list which would suggest that the television industry is doing a lot to help the youth of this country and the world. Perhaps the suggestion of Dr. Wilbur Schramm ought to be used to set the direction "I suggest that you do not think in terms of what television does *to* children, but rather, *what do children do with television?*" Therefore, perhaps it is useful to consider what youth does with television before we list what TV does to help them.

It seems that television is used by youth to entertain and inform them. They toy with it; it is mass culture; it is humor; it is small talk; it is "Did ya see...the other night?"; it is social, isolating, recreational, but, most of all, it simply IS. Television IS. That means it exists for today's American youth in a way foreign to those born before TV was a common resource.

Television in a minor way is an employer of youth, but of only a few of the vast number who need employment. Therefore, that is, not enough help. What does it do to help them on a loftier plane? Television is a developer of human potential; it helps us to know.

Jack Blessington is Director, Educational Relations CBS Television Network 51 West 52nd St, New York, 10019.

The Resource Of Television

Television is a vast transmitter of knowledge. It is one of youth's major informers. About what? About almost everything. It presents people, places and things. It presents foreign nations and common culture. It presents the arts, the sciences and the current issues of American and international life. It presents sports options, sports heroes and Olympic contests. It presents local, national and international news daily. It presents drama, humor, music, song, together with dance, photography, movies and documentaries. Television is journalistic, entertaining and enriching, while also being recreational, silly and playful. Youth, therefore, has access to all the educational potential that television offers.

Television as an industry does not set out to help youth as a primary goal. **As a commercial industry it operates within the framework of most responsible businesses in America and** cares about its employees and customers. Television does not exist outside of cultural or political realities but rather works within the context of a commercial industry. Commercial television is not, for example, educational television; it is not public broadcasting and it is not instructional television. While commercial television is all these in some manner, they are not the center of its life as an industry.

In looking back at the formative years of television which took place in America in the fifties, it seems the huge black and white consoles of the day were scarcely out of their packing cases before the naysayers descended. It would be several years until Newton Minnow would make his famous "vast wasteland" speech, but already, in 1959, it had become necessary for people such as Dr. Schramm to refute the myth that television was the primary cause of everything from the Crimean War to a growing lack of confidence in the Easter Bunny.

Today, television still has more than its fair share of detractors. This is especially true in the area of television's effect on children. Until someone can come forward with documentation that proves otherwise, as an educator, I suggest television is not anywhere near the primary problem with today's youngsters. Even if we were to throw every television set in America out the window, we would still have the major problems of poverty, mobility, value changes and changes in family life as well as political, racial and group tensions. Not only can television not be blamed for these major and evolutionary changes but, on the contrary, television can be credited with assisting us to recognize and manage the changes that swirl around us.

TELEVISION AND LITERACY

There are those who choose to believe that reading and literacy among young people were much more in evidence prior to the advent of television. Margaret Mead didn't agree with this assessment. In a 1973 Washington, D.C. speech to educators (3), she said many people like to believe that before the advent of television everyone sat around the table after dinner and had a wonderful conversation. She suggested that this was another myth in the making; there is no evidence to support the belief.

Rudolph Flesch also disagrees, "As I see it, children who are not taught to read in school at least learn a lot of things from TV. They enlarge their vocabulary and collect an unbelievable amount of information. Besides, it's sheer fantasy to think that if kids didn't watch TV they'd spend all those hours engrossed in good books (1)." ("Why Johnny Still Can't Read", *Family Circle*, November 1, 1979).

The recent and very constructive Ford study on adult illiteracy in the United States relates the problem clearly to the problems of poverty. It found that the social and economic structures of dominance, perpetuated in the schools, make it hard for many to learn. "In this country persons with limited education are often the same persons who suffer one or more of the major social disadvantages—poverty, unemployment, racial or ethnic discrimination, social isolation (2)." Those of us who have been in education for a long time know that it is poverty and not television that is the major culprit in the fight to overcome ignorance.

TELEVISION AND YOUTH

The problems and needs of youth are as many today as they have been throughout human history. There are unique problems waiting in the wings in the 1980's, just as there have always been problems throughout history which deserve the term "unique." Today's youth have to deal with energy problems, pollution, new styles of family life, longer life spans, longer and more compulsory formal education, the lessening of the dignity of manual labor, nuclear weapons, and the like.

Television provides youth with information about their world and, at times, the constructive advice of its elders for managing today's adversities. The problems of drugs and alcohol abuse are readily discussed along with information about biological sexuality and the affective nature of human relationships. Television presents the art, music, language, geography, politics and general culture of people in diverse parts of the world. This video encyclopedia helps our youth to know the world in less parochial terms than they might otherwise experience. This is essential learning for twentieth century life.

Television also presents many dramatic shows that help youth to look critically at prejudice, unreasonable anger, intolerance and impatience. From time to time, television also pokes fun at itself and this can help youth to view all media with a degree of healthy and respectful suspicion.

Television, it ought to be remembered, fits into a social setting and meets youth on the same road where youth meets the rest of life. The automobile, Concorde jet, computers, wonder drugs, synthetic fibers, laser technology, the miracles of science, the depth of religious faith and the profound realities of man's philosophies co-exist with television. Electronic music, vitamin pills and gerontology along with over-crowded schools and a lack of proper housing are all in the same world of youth. What is television doing for these aspects of the lives of youth—is that what we want to know?

Or is there a hidden statement? "Kids watch alot of television, perhaps too much—and what is TV doing to make sure that this generation does not arrive at their maturity in a state of diminished capacity?" As an educator, I entered the field of television because I think, as a technology and an industry, it is a great gift to twentieth century man. Put another way, it is twentieth century man's gift to himself. It is certainly the gifted inheritance of our human history and creative efforts and it is unmistakably a twentieth century benchmark.

Insofar as youth is concerned, the television industry is rather innocent. When people were initially excited about transmitting a video signal it is fair to guess they did not say, "What will this do for youth?" It is also fair to suggest that when television became the follow-up to the radio broadcasting industry it did not ask itself, "Will this help the youth of the world?" It just moved out into that era and dealt with man unsegregated by age categories. The view of youth and television needs a broader context and, together with Schramm, I think we can only approach it by asking: "How does youth experience television?"

TELEVISION AS ENVIRONMENT

As a former headmaster of two schools and the father of three college age students, I know that schooling, as I viewed it for youth and the way they experienced it, was vastly different. When my own children gather with friends to discuss their schooling, under my administration, I hardly recognize the institution, let alone the events. Schooling for the school-age youth is very different from schooling for their headmasters, professors or parents. The often studied television experiences of youth are, in my opinion, largely flawed. These studies attempt to tap the minds of the young, but the mind is difficult to examine, no matter how scientific and disciplined we are in our research.

Television, as environment, therefore, is different from television studied. Television is within the world of young people and their uses of it vary greatly. The intellectual, spiritual, psychic, moral and social development of youth as affected by television is worthy of study. But it is also very difficult to isolate this aspect of its reality. Youth is, after all, a part of the social system of parents, family, neighborhood, religion, school, diet, genetics, social class, race, general provincial culture, random chance and whatever else you can think of as an atmosphere.

To address and answer the initial topic of the television industry, I will say the curriculum of commercial television is vast and helpful. I know television is only a part of our culture and, although seemingly ever-present, it has only a relative effect on any one human. From my experiences, I believe television is a rather positive force for almost all youth.

While I wish to respect the concerns of parents and teachers regarding the potential distraction television may present to some children, it is not realistic to wish television would disappear. Television is not only here to stay, but commercial television is striving to be even more responsive and useful to both the educational and family life needs of the society. But commercial television is not instructional television; it enriches, but it is not a school.

Simply stated, I think the television industry helps youth by supplying them with vast amounts of information for knowing their world and dealing with it. The entertaining and fictional aspects of some of this information are easily processed by today's children—a generation born into a television society. They turn it into recreation. When it is fictional they know it is a contradiction to the other realities of their experience. They are at ease with television.

What the TV industry is doing to help youth opens up the whole area of what TV does for people in general. This is not the topic but I would feel it incomplete if I did not touch upon this broader topic. Almost every aspect of life is presented on television. Life and death, miracle medicine and malpractice, virtue and fraud in business, saints and sinners, heroes and villains, objective truths and fictions, the arts, the sciences, the faith and the doubt, are all presented. We lose our innocence when we lose our ignorance, as we also lose our prejudices. We lose our security as we see the world televised from the moon or from Iran, but we gain the brotherhood of man, the commonness of our fears and ways to cope. At the same time we are led to see the global, we see the microscopic, the small and sensitive aspect of our universe.

A peek at other people's families and their ways of dealing with stresses and burdens enables us to sense our own varied resources. We see and hear the symptoms of life's problems and we can recognize them more rapidly and respond more readily.

Television is obviously something man can deal with because for over thirty years he has been joyfully watching it. It has increased our memory, made greater and yet more common a world culture, it has joined us together with the horrors of wars and the joys of temporary peace, and we keep creating newer and more intriguing variations of our video capacity.

Our eyes are exercised by television to track multiactivities and our senses reach out to the artistic, creative and playful aspects of this modern medium.

Television is everyone's hometown newspaper, modern classroom, local Bijou theatre, voyeur's window, background fence, window on the world, UNESCO lecture and curious twentieth century phenomenon.

It is a friendly voice for some and an intruder for others but for most people, youth included, it is simply an informative and entertaining system of communication.

PROGRAMS FOR YOUTH

In a more immediate and school related sense, there is every indication that each of the networks has advanced greatly from the initial phase of simply transmitting signals. Programs such as CBS's *Captain Kangaroo, 30 Minutes,* and *The CBS Afternoon Playhouse,* ABC's *After School Specials,* and NBC's *Hot Hero Sandwich* and *Special Treat* are but a few of the many excellent hours of broadcasting geared to entertaining and educating today's youth. In addition, commercial television is offering more special news segments and full length news programs specifically designed to bring international, national and local events into perspective for young people. Local stations have joined in or led in this direction.

And all three networks are actively involved in bringing instructional guides for teachers into thousands of classrooms around the country. At CBS, we have three ongoing projects designed to utilize regular network programming to help improve students' reading skills.

The CBS Television Reading Program is a nationwide television script reading project that uses children's enthusiasm for television to help increase their motivation for further reading, learning and creative thinking.

As participants in the Reading Program (grades 4 through 12, depending on the subject matter of the particular broadcast), the students receive matched-to-broadcast scripts several weeks prior to the actual broadcast. The students work with the scripts in the classroom, often taking turns reading the various roles out loud. Their teachers also receive comprehensive Enrichment Guides which are used to initiate classroom discussions and involve the students in a variety of additional reading, writing and creative projects stemming from their work with the scripts. In the Reading Program, individual CBS affiliated stations work with local educators, newspapers and community-minded corporations in printing and distributing scripts to students. The scripts are also reproduced in the regular run of a number of major newspapers around the country in an effort to extend the script-reading to the entire community.

Since its inception three years ago, the Reading Program has already reached over 6,000,000 students. We think this helps our youth learn from television. More recently, CBS established the CBS/Library of Congress *Read More About It* book project and *The CBS Library Series.*

Read More About It is designed to encourage the public to read books by providing a bibliography on air after the program and lists sent to librarians comprised of titles related to specially selected CBS broadcasts. *The CBS Library Series* is special children's broadcasts which feature dramatizations of classic and contemporary books. All titles are chosen from the Library of Congress' annual list of recommended children's books. At the end of each broadcast, the program's host suggests to the children that they visit their local library and read the books from which the program's story was adapted.

The CBS Television Reading Program, the CBS/Library of Congress *Read*

More About It book project and *The CBS Library Series* are each a step forward in forging a new alliance between television and education. We think this helps young people and adults to learn while they are being entertained.

THE FUTURE

And what does the future hold? As more programs and projects of an educational nature are developed, as more broadcast research grants are forthcoming from foundations and the broadcasting industry itself, our youth learn more about the TV industry. And as more high schools, colleges, and graduate schools provide both theoretical and hands-on courses in the art of creating television programming, the term "television" will no longer be some ethereal mystery to America's youth and the industry will take another leap forward.

And then there's the electronic technology of the future. In the 1970's, television technology made more advancements in ten years than it had in the previous three decades combined. The 1980's will witness even more astonishing advancements. With the advent of the video disk and the continuing proliferation of cable and video cassette programming, the youth of America will have no choice but to become more varied in their viewing and uses of television. We are on the threshold of building a nation of more aware, more informed viewers.

The facts show that, despite its own youthfulness, the television industry is helping today's youth to know more about the world than any previous generation in human history.

1. Flesch, R. Why Johnny still can't read. *Family Circle,* November 1, 1979.

2. Hunter, St. J. and Harman, D. *Adult illiteracy in the United States: A report to the Ford Foundation.* New York: Mcgraw Hill Inc, 1979

3. Mead, M. paper presented to the National Association for Independent Schools, Washington, D.C., 1973.

SECTION V

The Environment of Educational Innovation: Schools and Teachers

This session addressed the problems of bringing about innovation change into the school. Ploghoft in his presentation stated the problem succinctly in wondering "(W)hy education in 1979 has not yet responded to major technological changes of the forties." The A&R sessions which followed these presentations were quite lively. The conferees, however, did come to agree that the school is the basic change unit and not the district or system. Top-down models of change are more likely to be resisted and subverted. Innovation begins with the teacher who, then, must be able to seek broad-based support and involvement from parents, administrative staff and curriculum specialists. Without this level of support innovative efforts will be limited to the classroom efforts of individual teachers. The district provides for the distribution of innovation but not its development.

What is Basic About Critical Receiver Skills?

Milton E. Ploghoft

INTRODUCTION

This paper discusses the prospects for curriculum development in the area of critical receiver skills that are relevant to television. It is with a special interest that I will consider such a curriculum's possibility in America's perennial "back to the basics" climate.

At the outset it is relevant to comment on the fact of other educational program developments, which like critical receiver skills, were prompted by social and technological changes. Economic education, consumer education, safety education, multicultural education, careers education, have not found smooth sailing by any means as their proponents have sought to gain a visible place for them in the K-12 curriculum. The resistance, or in most cases, disinterest in such curriculum developments can be attributed to a number of factors, not the least of which has been the lack of involvement of teachers and other school people in the development of the program concepts.

But the major obstacle to any curriculum change is the strongly entrenched belief that the basics take up so much time that there is really no

---

Milton E. Ploghoft is professor of curriculum and instruction at Ohio University; he was one of the Co-Directors of the conference.

way that newly emerging curriculum content can be accommodated. This belief appears to be as strong among educators as it is among the general citizenry. If we consider the impact of minimal competency testing we can better understand why teachers are cautious about taking on additional curricular responsibilities. If the teachers are to be evaluated in terms of how well their pupils perform on tests in reading, writing and arithmetic, we should not be suprised that the lion's share of teaching time will be spent on those "basics."

Action has now been taken by legislatures and departments of education in more than 40 states to require children to pass minimal competency tests at designated grade levels as a pre requistite to promotion and graduation. It is not my intent to here argue the merits of such requirements, but I am convinced that these actions are not conducive to curriculum innovations. It is more than ironic that in some states there appears to be no official interest in the student's preparation to accept the responsibility involved in being an American citizen. In such situations can you imagine any ground swells of support for critical receiver skills in the curriculum?

FIFTY YEARS BEHIND

Perhaps it is for these and other reasons that the futurists in education keep their eyes directed toward the year 2020, rather than trying to figure out why education in 1979 has not yet responded to major technological changes of the forties. Futurism of this sort is simple. We catalog the problems and concerns of today and then wisely predict that education will respond to these concerns about 50 years hence.

Such is the case with television. Since shortly after World War II, television has penetrated America, rapidly and completely. Television has pushed aside reading as the major medium of one way mass communication. And television, much like the automobile, has become the object of a love-hate relationship with America's people.

And so, as adult Americans spend more than 20 hours week viewing the football games, the soap operas, the sexy films, and the saucy sit-coms, we fret that our children are not reading enough, are not getting enough exercise are not being brought up on the good old moral values that put us where we are today—in a soft chair with a can of beer—in front of the television set.

In spite of the almost constant clamor that has been raised since the early 50's regarding television's effect upon our children—the studies by the surgeon generals' office, by the congress, by this group and that group—we should not expect that critical receivership skills will gain ready access to the curriculum of our schools. We have not found time for many other programs that seemed to hold high merit. Things have to be *basic* to take root and grow in the elementary curriculum. Things have to prepare you for college or a job to take root and grow in the high school. Critical receiver skills can promise none of these. It appears that the conventional view of *basic* has never referred to survival skills in a democracy.

RECEIVERSHIP SKILLS ARE BASIC

But, could it be that critical receivership skills are, in and of themselves *basic*,—not only to one's sane existence in todays' world—but *basic* in the sense that they are made up of the observational and listening skills that are fundamental to total language development? Could it be that receiver skills are actually the first R? Long overlooked, long disregarded in our narrow treatment of language development?

I shall attempt to explain myself, and in the process, suggest why critical receiver skills may fare better than many other curriculum prospects of the last 20-30 years.

We know that television is the medium that uses the spoken work, non-verbal languages and an infinite array of visual and sound effects to communicate the messages of the programming.

Television uses the language that is natural to the human. Children, shortly after birth, are able to begin receiving and responding to the language of television. The child's early encounters with non-verbal cues and her use of oral communication, long before the printed symbol carries any meaning for her, is most compatible with the communicative medium of television.

Television uses the natural language that communicates the major elements of a culture. The characters of television express happiness, sadness, anger and grief to children regardless of the reading level of the young viewers.

It is through interpersonal communication, using the oral language, that children acquire information concerning the behavior of the people in home and neighborhood. Before the child encounters reading as an avenue to an infinite array of vicarious experiences, she has begun to develop her own concepts of right and wrong, love and hate, friend and stranger from perceptions of the behavior around her.

Special meaning is given to gestures, facial expressions, subtle actions as well as to tone of voice and manners of speaking. Long before the child encounters reading, she has found that many of her needs to comprehend can be satisfied through the use of oral language and a discriminating perception of people and actions. Television content imparts meaning in this manner.

A common complaint of reading teachers has been to the effect that "poor readers" have not had adequate language background, that they are inattentive listeners, that skill in visual discrimination is lacking, that the poor reader can not organize into logical sequence a series of events in a story. We find here a list of related characteristics that are basic to success in reading. And we find here a number of the skills that are essential to the effective use of television content, whether that content is entertainment, informational or commercial.

The language of television is basic, it is natural and it would be utter nonsense to hope or expect that it would not be appealing to human beings who want to find out what is going on with other people.

Paul Witty, writing in 1939, commented on the state of the language development program in the schools.

> Accustomed to talking throughout the day (using perhaps 30,000 words per day) the youngster wants and needs to talk about all the new and interesting experiences which are found in school. Instead we try to channel his language through the written word. It is small wonder that this reading and writing come to be thought of as bars to learning rather than opportunities, (1, p. 17).

It seems reasonable to observe that, in our long standing preoccupation with the mechanics of reading, we have neglected the very language foundations which are essential to success in reading and to total language development. And in our zeal to get the youngsters to read at grade level, we have not dared to take the time to attend to the antecedent conditions that relate so closely to reading achievement.

Forty years after witty the schools find themselves entangled in minimal competency requirements that reinforce the long standing neglect of total language development. But a major *technological* change in communication media has occurred and we are now well into a communications revolution. It seems that this fact is recognized generally with the possible exception of our school programs.

Whether we in education want to accept the awesome impact of television upon our ways of living, we cannot deny that the skills needed to deal effectively and critically with this new medium are basic language skills. And with our nation's traditional commitment to the basics, we should be able to develop critical viewing skills programs without being accused of introducing fads and frills.

So we could be half way along to resolving the question of how to accomplish curricular intervention for critical viewing (receiver) skills. Since these skills are basic language skills and since they provide the underpinning for the reading process, we can address two problems with a careful reordering of priorities in the language development program of the school. And it would appear that we can use television programs as content for our work in this very basic skill development.

Let us consider, at least briefly, four of the five major skill areas that Anderson and I (2, p. 8-13) have identified as constituting the core of critical receiver skills relevant to understanding the televised message.

> *Comprehending the message* which includes specifying the working element of the message, interpreting the intent of the message, and comprehending images and language discriminently.
>
> *Perceiving the elements of the messages* which includes perceiving relationships among these elements, noting sequence of events, identifying character traits, noting the integration of aural and visual effects.

Evaluation of the message which includes assignment of credibility to statements, identifying affective appeals, identifying fact, opinion, imaginative writing, and identifying logic and reason in the message. *Reacting to the message personally* which includes drawing conclusions, relating other experiences to the message, relegating value to the message, and recognizing emotional satisfactions gained from the message.

Receiver skills appropriate for use in television viewing can be approached in *school* situations where rather conventional instructional materials are being used. A common primary level unit in language arts involves children in activities such as:

Learning to listen
Telling a story about a picture
Picture sequence
Interpreting pictures

other units include:

Building sentences that tell who did it.
Building sentences that tell when and where.

It appears that such activities can be based upon viewing some type of television program content. Even at the primary level, a TV commercial can be viewed as a listening and observing activity. By third and fourth grade, TV commercials can be viewed with the sound turned down and children can create the "stories" that they think should go with the pictures.

Children can view all or a portion of an entertainment program and then write their own endings, or they may watch an entire program and write an alternative ending.

Basic language skills can be brought into use as we use televised content that is familiar to children. And as young viewers learn to "interrogate" the television content, they may establish receiver habits that are basic to critical viewing.

In the middle grades and junior high school it is not uncommon to involve children in writing book reports. An excellent preparatory activity would have the students view a television entertainment program for the purpose of identifying main characters, minor characters, and characters that were not needed to carry the plot forward.

As young students work with the television content, they will develop skills of observation and analysis that will be useful when they are asked to write a review of a book they have read.

It is important that we recognize that analysis of television content is a valid and pertinent learning activity in its own right. The foregoing comments illustrate the integral relationships that exist between conventional approaches and mediated approaches.

The experiences in Eugene, East Syracuse, and Idaho Falls offer early evidence that these major skill areas can be developed within the framework of existing programs in the language arts and social studies areas. I would predict that the basic nature of these skill areas will strengthen the prospects for success of viewing skills in the curriculum of our schools.

It will be most necessary that *we* understand—first—that *we* are dealing with basics that support total language growth. If we can not communicate the real character of critical receiver skills as being basic, we will fight a losing battle, with educators and lay people alike.

I believe that it is necessary to be quite honest with ourselves with respect to the "basics" in the curriculum, particularly with respect to reading as it relates to our concerns with television. We need to recognize the very real possibility that we have committed ourselves so completely to reading as the only avenue to true education that we have become unable to consider the changing conditions and the need for alternative educational responses.

In this regard I believe that we must avoid treating television as a stepping stone to better reading, rather than as a medium which deserves and requires educational attention in its own right. I do not accuse any person or any group of intentional deception on this point, but I am convinced that we will only compound our long neglect of total language development if we use television as a sugar pill to induce reading.

It is useful to recognize the monumental contributions of the print medium to the institutions of reading and later to the realization of the age of science and technology. But in this recognition, we need not bow before the god of reading to the exclusion of all other avenues to learning.

It will not come easily for American education to recognize, in the universal use of television, the need to re-examine and to re-design our programs in language development. In spite of the evidence before us, we should not expect a widespread acknowledgement of the most basic nature of the language skills that are appropriate to critical uses of television. Television has been around for only 30 years. General educational responses may take another decade or two.

If our programs in education are to be even vaguely responsive to the problems brought by our uses of television, we will need publishers and producers of instructional materials to take part in the break with print tradition. We must have language development programs that make greater use of mediated materials. We must make far greater use of contemporary television program content in our language development efforts.

Evaluation of student learning must make use of mediated material in the content of the instruments. Our own minimal competencies must be expanded to recognize the basic character of language skills in addition to reading.

The nature of the educational problems related to television must become the subject of much more through study and discussion by professional and citizen groups. In this regard, I think it is accurate to say that a continuing preoccupation with the question: "What does television do to us?" will prove to be a road block to us as we consider educational programs that respond to the question: "How can we prepare people to become critical users of television?" We must recognize that we are victims of a new technology only if we are willing to be.

Critical receiver skills, or critical viewing skills, as an area of curriculum innovation and development will be integrated into educational programs only to the extent that education and citizens view them as basic to the *traditional* goals of the schools. Critical receiver skills relevant to television will not gain a curriculum home on the grounds that *contemporary* social conditions require them to be taught. Social Studies, long said to provide the citizenship education so vital to our democracy are now down to 35 minutes per week of class time in our elementary schools according to a recent study by Dick Gross of Stanford.

Implementation and institutionalization of curriculum changes are far more complex than is the conceptualization and designing of programs that respond to changes in our world. The many federally funded social studies projects of the sixties left a small legacy to the social studies programs of the seventies. And where innovation was sustained, it seemed to be due to the incorporation of the new elements into conventional text materials.

The work that many of you have begun in this area is indeed important—but perhaps too few of us know that. A great portion of our public may think that TV means no more than entertainment and why should the schools take time with this?

I believe that our contributions to curriculum development will rise or fall to the extent that critical receiver skills are understood and accepted as basic elements in total language proficiency. So, as we go, let us stay close to the basics in the knowledge that receiver skills begins with an *R*.

REFERENCES

1. Paul A. Witty and C. Skinner, *Mental Hygiene in Modern Education*, New York: Farrer and Rinehart, 1949. p. 17

2. Milton E. Ploghoft and James A. Anderson, "Television Receivership Skills: The new Social Literacy." *Social Science Record*, Winter 1977, 8-13.

Critical Receivership Skills: The Need For Innovation at the Local School District Level

James F. Parsley Jr.

INTRODUCTION

Few topics in our society today engender as much diversity of opinion as does the topic of television and its effects upon children. One may agree with Marshall McLuhan that television extends man's environment or one may place little credence on the effects of television. Increasingly, however, parents and teachers are beginning to realize that television is the most powerful medium of communication and that school may actually be secondary in importance in shaping the lives of young people.

For more than a decade, society has grown more dependent upon television as a provider of information. Television has displaced older media as a primary source of information for the majority of citizens in our society. Television is viewed in nearly 95 percent of America's homes. None of these developments, however, are particularly new or surprising to any one present in this room today. For nearly twenty years, research evidence has indicated that children have the greatest trust in what they see and hear on television as compared to the printed word (C). Despite the fact that our experience now spans well over three decades in terms of wide scale public usage of television,

---

James F. Parsley Jr. is Superintendent of Schools, Idaho Falls Schools District 91. The system was the location of the Idaho critical receivership skills project.

American education has just now started to admit to an awareness of the pervasive effects of television.

Unfortunately, American education has been extremely slow to pick up the challenge. At its best, American education has proven its competence in the teaching basic skills needed for language development and numeric reasoning. As an innovator, however, American education stands indicted as being largely tradition oriented and unresponsive to change. Many educational observers are troubled that despite massive federal spending to promote innovation in education, there has been little impact indeed. Even with massive federal expenditures, two decades of educational innovation have not produced pervasive change in the classrooms of America.

Neil Postman, suggests that schooling is completely organized around pre-electronic patterns of communication. "Because of its tradition-bound content, school is old times and old bias (5, p. 163)." He further postulates that the value of schooling is merely to give a child a sense of perspective. He states that by putting television and school side by side, we can see where we are going (television) and what we are leaving (schooling). I, for one, find Postman's analogy most disturbing. One can get the same historical perspective by visiting a museum and observing the fossils of a bygone era. Perhaps the real issue before educators and parents today is not whether the television media should be recognized as an educator of children, but rather whether there will be a place for American schools in our brave new electronic world.

Rationale For The Teaching Of Critical Receivership Skills

Some of you would perhaps agree with me that our public schools essentially do a good job of teaching the basic skills of language and mathematics literacy. The "report card" however, is less favorable on the ability or effort of American schools to teach the more complex thinking skills. These "critical thinking skills" briefly can be stated as including knowledge of the nature of valid inferences, abstractions, generalizations, syllogistic reasoning, propaganda analysis, and varied activities and phases of problem solving (1). Whether these skills, once taught, are the same for televised content and the printed page is not altogether certain.

At its best, television offers a number of unique advantages which tend to make content more meaningful: it is available to those who are not proficient in the skills of reading; it can present information which sound or print alone could not capture; it offers a dimension of reality not encountered in print; and, it has an unparalleled potential to bring the emotion of an event to the viewer.

When contrasted to printed media, however, not all of television's characteristics seem favorable for the critical analysis of content: it lacks referability; its speed of presentation is not controlled by the viewer; and, it requires concentration throughout the presentation of the message (7). For some time now, there has been concern that the mass media, and television in particular, are passively absorbed with little opportunity for critical reaction (3). Despite such concern, schools have essentially chosen to ignore any special implications as a result of television's unique characteristics.

Accompanying the growth and influence of commercial television has been very little recognition among educators regarding the lack of critical reaction and interaction afforded in the televiewing of children and adolescents.

For almost a decade, America's educators have also been indifferent to some rather notable educational futurists as they have called for more and better analysis of propaganda and the development of critical thinking about mass media content (2).

That the traditional school curriculum is oriented to printed and spoken communication is evident. The acquisition of language stresses decoding and encoding skills in regard to written and spoken language. Additionally, some emphasis is placed upon listening skills in the elementary schools. School curriculum contains a built-in "scope" and "sequence" inherently contained in a textbook approach. This structure is also one of the strongest educational tools known to educators as instructional material is organized into coherent patterns beginning with simple concepts and progressing to the more abstract. Ideally, a school curriculum also contains elements of correlation between subject matter and articulation between grade levels. Conversely television is multi-dimensional and while definite elements of organization or structure hold together a single program (or, to some degree, a long-running television series) the overall content of television is widely disparate. Formal education traditionally has been interactive in nature with the classroom teacher as the key disseminator of information. Television content as a whole is highly fragmented with little opportunity for interaction of any kind, yet the potential for emotional affect is extremely high.

There has been an *a prior* assumption that the skills emphasized in our nation's schools are sufficient to equip students to interpret and make discriminating judgments about television programs, newscasts, commercials, and documentaries. Upon examination, it is evident that public education has not been up to this particular challenge and that, in fact, schools today are doing little, if anything, to equip students to be discerning consumers of televised communications or to develop "critical thinking skills" in general.

Commercial television spends millions of dollars on the effort to manipulate audience attitudes and behaviors. The average school-age child witnesses several hundred thousand television commercials between the ages of 5 and 18. Again, educators and parents have simply assumed that the skills taught in the schoolhouse are sufficient to equip children to become discriminating viewers and consumers in the market place. Such an assumption, in my opinion, is groundless. The average graduating senior today has experienced approximately 11,000 hours of classroom instruction compared to an average of 15,000 hours of television instruction via commercial programming. The effects of this instruction are largely unknown and unmeasurable by educators partly because of an attitude of indifference toward this new electronic educational institution.

In summary, there is a serious void in the development of critical thinking skills which enhance the ability of students to interpret and make discriminating judgements about television content. Educators have largely assumed something like a "Maginot Line" philosophy in assuming that television is merely for the "entertainment" of children. Television's importance as an educational institution requires both recognition and educational response. Clearly, there is strong rationale and need for innovative educational programs in the development of critical televiewing or "receivership" skills. It is also evident that change in American education is difficult to achieve and that if such change is to be meaningful it must reach into the classroom and into the very curriculum being offered in those classrooms.

Supporting Innovation At The Local School District Level

What are the implications for supporting innovation at the school district level? Even with the admission of its inevitability, there is still a tendency on the part of many people to resist change. Many educators would like to assume that life and the institutions that have been established can continue without significant change in traditional patterns or procedures. It is true that for some, change will occur with or without coordinated planning. Assuming, however, that educators are to be part of that change, rather than casual observers of a passing parade of federally funded programs, it would seem that a few key elements must be present.

It is essential that greater attention be focused on research and development as it relates to the effects and dynamics of commercial television. In short, curriculum needs to be developed which fosters the teaching of critical thinking skills and critical televiewing skills. Desperately needed is the preservation of an innovative climate which allows for the pitfalls of "trial and error" and experimentation. Unfortunately, American education is currently running in a trend counter to such a climate. Increased pressure is mounting for a "return to the basics" and for a renewed commitment to traditional ways. This should have some profound implications for project design and for funding applications.

The need for educational leadership is evident. Educational leaders need to understand and to accept the rationale for change. They must, in turn, be able to mobilize education and to cause planning and curriculum change in their own districts.

Also, the role of the state superintendent of public instruction is vital as it relates to the development of a curriculum which is responsive to the teaching of televiewing skills. Chief state school officers represent an important group of individuals that can have impact throughout our nation's schools. It is important that support and assistance be garnered from the various state departments of education.

Additionally, presenters from this particular conference and some of the projects herein highlighted should participate at the national conferences of the American Association of School Administrators and the National School Boards Association. These are conferences attended by upwards of 10,000 to 15,000 people and they have profound impact on the governance of our nation's schools.

In addition, an important element supporting innovation at the local school district level is the involvement of people. When both lay citizens and educators have an opportunity to become involved in the problems and needs of our changing society they will bring new perspectives and insights and will, in turn, be supportive of needed change. Another element conducive to local innovation is the identification and mobilization of community resources. Any innovative curricular program is highly dependent upon key people that bring to the project special qualifications, interests, and talents essential to successful change. As it relates to the creation of a new curricular thrust involving televiewing or receivership skills, key community resource people may well be found in the local media itself.

I want to disagree respectfully with my colleague who indicated that, "decision making at the local level results sometimes in inertia." I would say that "a *lack* of decision-making at the local level results in inertia." Parent involvement no longer is an option for the educator, it is a requirement. In order for any receivership program to succeed, parent involvement will need to be an integral part of program design and implementation. Education in general must cause a renewed alliance and relationship between the home and the school.

Receivership skills ideally should be integrated with existing curriculum, preferably in the language arts and social studies area. Integration with existing curriculum will allow for practical application and soundness of curricular approach. Infusion into the existing curriculum is essential! In developing a curricular thrust in critical receivership or critical thinking, you must be very careful to avoid new, exotic and pedantic language. When you deal with lay citizens and board members it is *your* obligation to present understandable language. It is not their obligation to purchase a *Roget's Thesaurus,* or to take a course in "graduation research design" at Teachers College.

Another essential ingredient for innovation at the local level is the continuing support which must be provided to project staff. Support needs to be put in a tangible sense with evidence that the district recognizes the importance of the effort and has a commitment to the project's success.

Critical receivership programs need to be adapted with hardware and materials now available in the schools. There is a limitation in public education funds at the present time and most local districts cannot afford to implement a curricular thrust which requires a great deal of new equipment, hardware and machinery.

There should be a linkage with the current cycle of federally funded projects now working on critical televiewing skills. There needs to be a commitment on the part of the project people to meet perhaps a year from now and to share information with one another. That is the best way to maximize limited public funds which are available for this type of effort. Also, there should be a commitment to share tapes and printed materials from these projects.

Educational innovation must feature ongoing product and process evaluation. Summative evaluation is highly important in determining the outcome or product of the innovative effort. Additionally, formative evaluation is the key to the successful operation of the project as it allows a project to continually assess its efforts and to provide for redirection and improvement throughout the operational effort.

In order for there to be significant change in the classrooms of America, innovative efforts must be eventually infused into the educational mainstream. Innovative programs need to be demonstrated and implemented within the educational community. The development of a strategy for change at the local school district level is highly dependent on board commitment, administrative leadership skills and the overall educational climate. The best strategy for each community will undoubtedly be tailored according to the unique needs and conditions located therein.

References

1. Ennis, R. A definition of critical thinking. In Richard E. Ripple (ed.), *Readings in learning and human abilities: Educational psychology.* New York: Harper and Row Publishers, 1964.

2. Kenworthy, L. *Guide to social studies teaching.* Belmont, California: Wadsworth Publishing Company Inc., 1970, 3d ed.

3. Mills, G.W. *The power elite.* London: Oxford University Press, 1956.

4. Parsley, J.F. Jr. A comparison of the ability of ninth grade students to apply several critical thinking skills to problematic content presented through two different media. Unpublished doctor's dissertation, Ohio University, Athens, Ohio 1970.

5. Postman, N. The first curriculum: Comparing school and television. *Phi Delta Kappan,* 1979, *61* (3), 163.

6. Schramm, W. Lyle, J. and Parker, E.B. *Television in the lives of our children.* Stanford, California: Stanford University Press, 1961.

7. Travers, R.M.W. *et al. Research and theory to audio-visual information transmission.* U.S. Department of Health, Education and Welfare, Contract No. 3-20-003, 1967.

THE ROLE OF TEACHER EDUCATION IN INNOVATION AND CHANGE

Bob G. Woods

STRATEGIES FOR INTRODUCING EDUCATIONAL CHANGE THROUGH TEACHER EDUCATION

There is a growing body of knowledge that clearly indicates the importance of television upon the social, moral and cognitive development of our nation's children. The problem with which we are confronted is how to capitalize upon this body of knowledge in providing improved educational opportunities for young people both at home and in our schools. My concern in this paper is the role of teacher education in curricular innovation and change with respect to the teaching of television receivership skills and the body of knowledge related to television as an educational vehicle. The major focus of the paper is on the processes of bringing about significant changes in teacher education programs to include a new dimension or a new emphasis, in this case, the knowledge and skills related to television as a medium of instruction for children and youth.

The antecedents of curricular change and the improvement of instruction in elementary and secondary schools are change and improvement in teacher education—both inservice and preservice. Inservice teacher education programs may be provided in a variety of ways—teacher centers, programs

---

Bob G. Woods is Dean of the College of Education, University of Missouri.

planned and conducted by local education agencies, programs conducted by state educational or regional educational laboratories, and programs offered by the teacher education units of institutions of higher education. Although their leadership status is being threatened; schools, departments, and colleges of education in institutions of higher education still play the dominant role in teacher education at both the preservice and inservice levels. This being the case, what do teacher education units need to do to prepare teachers who are competent in teaching television receivership skills and in making optimum use of television as a vehicle for educational improvement?

If a new or different body of knowledge and set of skills are to be incorporated into a teacher education program, the teacher trainers, needless to say, have to be qualified to implement the change. Often this necessitates the hiring of new personnel possessing the desired competencies or providing a faculty development program for the teacher trainers. Because of current budgetary constraints in institutions of higher learning due to declining student enrollments and other factors, the most feasible approach is through a faculty development program. Although this appears simple enough, conducting faculty development programs that are effective for college faculties has not been a common practice. College professors are not easily convinced of the need for curricular innovations, and, even if they are receptive to change, they are reluctant to commit the time to engage in such programs. Notwithstanding the fact that teaching is the most important function of most colleges and universities, relatively little time and effort are devoted to making it more effective and efficient. Therefore, faculty development programs for teacher educators must be carefully planned and implemented if they are to be successful.

FACULTY DEVELOPMENT: A GROWING NEED

In the past, attending meetings of professional organizations and occasionally participating in special workshops or institutes have comprised the faculty development activities of most professors of teacher education. However, a number of societal and economical conditions today are creating an unprecedented need for faculty development programs in teacher education institutions. Declining enrollments in schools, colleges, and departments of education are causing the deletion of positions on teacher education faculties, which result in the addition of fewer new faculty members than is normal. In short, without the infusion of so-called "new blood," teacher education faculties in most institutions are growing simultaneously both older and obsolescent. Faculty development programs are a desirable approach to counteract this growing malady.

The rapid increase in the knowledge base, sometimes referred to as a "knowledge explosion," and the development and use of a more sophisticated educational technology also create a genuine need for faculty retooling. It is not uncommon to find school systems employing technical equipment and instructional systems that are more advanced than those used in the teacher education institutions from which they employ their beginning teachers. Elementary and secondary school faculties often are more sophisticated and knowledgeable about educational technology than are teacher education faculties.

Although there is an obvious need for faculty development programs in teacher education institutions today, they are not always easy to initiate. The reward system for faculty members in colleges and universities, for example, particularly in the larger institutions, favors the individuals who are engaged in research and publication. Therefore, time devoted to faculty development programs focusing on curricular change and the improvement of instruction distract one from what he or she perceives as being more important from the standpoint of both professional and monetary rewards. Whether we are sympathetic with it or not, the "publish or perish" syndrome is with us today as strongly as it ever has been.

BASIC ASSUMPTIONS

The climate for introducing change varies considerably from one situation to another because of the many variables involved. In any case, after an analysis of the situation, the undergirding basic assumptions upon which the faculty development program is to built should be identified. Based upon past experience in introducing new content into teacher education curricula, the assumptions that would be applicable to most teacher education programs in which television receivership skills and the related body of knowledge are to be incorporated are as follows:

1. Changes in teacher education programs with respect to content and/or structure do not occur rapidly, thus implementing significant changes will be a slow process.

2. Members of the faculty will exhibit differing degrees of interest in the various activities of the faculty development program; therefore, it is not realistic to expect all members of the faculty to participate in all inservice activities.

3. Some faculty members philosophically will be opposed to or in disagreement with the proposed changes and will resist any changes affecting their courses.

4. Most teacher educators are knowledgeable about conducting successful inservice programs for public school personnel, but they are not particularly adept at conducting or actively participating in inservice projects for college faculties.

5. Voluntary participation in inservice activities will be more productive in bringing about change than required or coerced participation.

6. Faculty development programs will be more effective if faculty members are delegated an important role in planning and implementing the programs.

7. Faculty involvement in faculty development programs will enhance by administrative encouragement and support.

8. Involvement of public school teachers and administrators in planning and conducting some of the inservice activities will enhance the success of the faculty development program.

9. A successful faculty development program has an evaluation component that provides information about its effectiveness and subsequent needed modifications.

A major assumption upon which this presentation is based is that the change which is needed in teacher education involves more than assigning a member of the faculty to teach a course on critical viewing skills. For optimum effectiveness, all or at least a major portion of the teacher education faculty need to be cognizant of the body of knowledge related to teaching critical viewing skills to children and youth. Pertinent aspects of this knowledge should permeate methods courses, courses focusing on learning, and courses on child growth and development and should not be restricted to a single course.

IMPLEMENTING A FACULTY DEVELOPMENT PROGRAM

Faculty development programs for the implementation of curricular change may be thought of as having distinct stages. According to Wood, Thompson, and Russell in their treatise on inservice education, there are five stages which include Readiness, Planning, Training, Institutionalization, and maintenance. (1) In this paper the overall process will be compressed into three stages—awareness, training, and implementation. The 1978 *Rand Study* describes the process by which an innovation is translated into an operating reality with school districts as having three overlapping phases, i.e., mobilization, implementation, and institutionalization (2, p. 13).

Developing *awareness*, the first stage of a faculty development program, may be thought of as the process of fostering an understanding of the need for change and a commitment to a new set of professional behaviors. In this case, the focus is on the need to prepare teachers to teach television receivership skills or critical viewing skills. Teacher educators may or may not be cognizant of this specialized body of knowledge and skills, and, even if they are informed, they might not be receptive to making changes in the courses they teach. Attitudinal change, therefore, is often an important aspect of the first phase of a faculty development project.

Basic to any effort directed toward the development of awareness is the dissemination of pertinent information. A faculty development program focusing on television receivership skills and the related body of knowledge is no exception. According to Ploghoft and Anderson, (3, p. 10), "There is a fair-sized body of literature relating television's effects on the cognitive, social, moral, and behavioral development of the child." A variety of ways may be employed to familiarize faculty members with this literature. Among the more effective ways are assembling a collection of the relevant materials and making them available to the teachers. The development of a bibliography of research reports and other pertinent materials which can be procured and circulated or otherwise made available to the faculty is an important strategy. In addition to research reports, articles in professional journals, and books, various types of instructional materials should be collected for the perusal of the faculty.

Faculty seminars conducted by outside consultants or knowledgeable faculty members are another way of disseminating information, creating an awareness of new knowledge, and stimulating an interest in curricular change. The effectiveness of this technique depends largely upon the degree to which the consultant relates his/her presentation and contributions to the particular instructional setting. Seminar presentations and discussions are facilitated by distributing a paper on the subject or other pertinent materials prior to the seminar session.

A faculty retreat is another means of developing an awareness of the need **for curricular change and** perhaps a readiness to launch into a program of curricular development and instructional improvement. The effectiveness of the retreat will depend largely on the extent to which the program is carefully planned in advance. The program might consist of keynote speakers and reaction panels, demonstrations, small-group discussions, and work sessions designed to obtain wide-spread participation. The program for the retreat must be made interesting and/or provocative or the attendance will be disappointing.

The utilization of evaluation instruments will yield valuable information as to the degree to which the faculty develops an awareness of the need to incorporate instruction in television receivership skills and related information in teacher education curricula. It should be pointed out, however, that evidence of awareness on the part of the teacher education faculty does *not* indicate a commitment to introduce change in one's teaching.

The College of Education, University of Missouri-Columbia, is now in its fifth year of an intensive faculty development program focusing on improving faculty competence for preparing teachers to teach handicapped children in regular classrooms—to implement P.L. 94-142. The Education for All Handicapped Children Act. Support for the program has been provided by the Bureau for the Education of the Handicapped, U.S. Office of Education under its Dean's Grant Program. At the end of the first year and a half, the evaluation data showed that the faculty had developed a positive awareness of P.L. 94-142 and of the need to make substantive changes in their teacher education courses in order to prepare teachers who are equipped to successfully teach handicapped children in regular classrooms. Yet, the data also clearly showed that very little actually was being done to attain this goal. A "firing of the gun" was needed according to the outside evaluation specialist to move the faculty development program into the next stage—the actual training or acquisition of the knowledge and skills needed to make the pertinent changes in the teacher education program (4, p. 63-69).

Conducting a needs assessment survey to determine the current level of knowledge and skill of the faculty is a useful first-step in the *training stage*. With reference to the topic at hand, the survey should determine to what extent members of the faculty are informed about the body of knowledge related to teaching critical viewing skills.

A variety of approaches may be utilized to provide the training needed by the teacher education faculty. Workshops focusing on critical viewing skills which are planned and conducted by competent people probably will prove to be both popular with participants and generally effective.

Study by faculty members at another institution that is more advanced in teaching critical viewing skills can be an effective procedure. Other strategies include visitation, simulations, or on-the-job experiences at a school that teaches critical viewing skills. Firsthand experience as an observer and as a participant are conductive to producing changed behavior. Regardless of the learning activity in which one engages, it is important to reinforce the newly acquired knowledge and skills by providing opportunities to build relationships and to communicate with one's fellow participants.

An effective strategy that has been used effectively in the Dean's Grant Project at the University of Missouri-Columbia focusing on techniques of the handicapped children in regular classrooms is the appointment of selected faculty members to serve as "faculty facilitators." The role of the facilitator is to provide suggestions, printed and audio-visual instructional materials, research reports and related literature, and more important of all, encouragement. The facilitator plans inservice activities and promotes communication among faculty members. Faculty facilitators are rewarded with released time, secretarial assistance, materials allotment, special travel allotment, or some other perquisite.

Recognition is also an effective stimulant. Acknowledgement of the accomplishments of the participants as well as the facilitators, reinforces interest and stimulates motivation. If properly chosen and rewarded, the facilitators become strong advocates for change. They regard curricular development and instructional improvement as a personal and professional challenge.

The third stage of a faculty development program focusing on curricular development and/or instructional improvement is *implementation*—putting the new or revised program into operation and taking measures to assure that it remains in operation until it is fully institutionalized. An advisory committee comprised of faculty members and administrators, selected early in the faculty development project, should be involved in planning the implementation stage. Having a stake in planning curricular change is tantamount to making a commitment to support the change.

The plan for implementation should have a statement of objectives, a time-table for effecting change, and built-in system of evaluation. A budget to purchase materials and provide for other needs is essential to the success of the project. Technical assistance also should be made available as needed to cope with unanticipated problems. Technical assistance might be obtained from an external educational agency or professional educator as well as from the local staff.

It is not uncommon for a curricular innovation or change to get off to a good start only to be abandoned at a later date. The 1978 *Rand Study* for the U.S. Office of Education provides much evidence to support this statement (5, p.9). The complete and full institutionalization of a significant curricular change requires a continuous program of maintenance. There seems to be a natural tendency to revert to former practices if the change or innovation is left unattended.

The status leaders of the faculty are key to the success of implementing curricular innovation and change. A disinterested or indifferent departmental chairperson or dean can play havoc with any faculty development program focusing on curricular change. If, on the other hand, the status leaders—dean and departmental chairpersons—remove obstacles to the implementation of the program and provide, encouragement, the faculty will attach greater importance to the project and devote increased effort to their work (6, p. 31). Personal involvement in the faculty development program focusing on curricular change on the part of the leader(s) conveys to the members of the faculty the importance attached to the project. It should be pointed out, however, that the effectiveness of leadership will be enhanced when based on competence and knowledge related to the project goals rather than by status of position alone.

An evaluation plan contributes to institutionalizing curricular change. Data are needed to determine the extent to which the critical competencies have been learned by the teacher education students. If the evaluation data do not indicate the desired results, adjustments can be made. If they indicate success, knowledge of this fact is stimulating to faculty members. The absence of evaluative data, however, creates apprehension, doubt, and/or indifference.

Evaluation of our senior's knowledge and skills for implementing P.L. 94-142 is one of the major components of our Dean's Grant Project at UMC this year. We are fully cognizant, however, that student outcomes do not tell the whole story of the success or lack of success of a curricular development project. Changes in the teaching style of faculty members for example, are an important project outcome in their own right.

In our Dean's Grant Project at UMC, a list of "critical competencies," focusing on the preparation of teachers for the implementation of P.L. 94-142 was developed by the faculty under the direction and leadership of the project coordinator and the faculty facilitators. The chairpersons of the Department of Curriculum and Instruction and the Department of Special Education used the list of critical competencies with their respective faculties to determine in which courses the various competencies should be taught and whether or not they actually were being taught. This was a very useful exercise for effecting curricular change and assigning content responsibilities. If the evaluation data indicate that certain competencies are not being attained by the teacher education students, it is relatively easy to determine where or in which courses the breakdown is occurring. The development of critical competencies for teaching receivership skills would be useful in bringing about needed changes in teacher education.

SUMMARY

In summary, there are many factors that serve as deterrants to curricular innovation and change in our schools. Among these are philosophical bias of school officials and/or the public, tradition, faculty lethurgy, crowded curricula, lack of public interest and support, lack of an adequate knowledge base, and inadequate or inappropriate teacher education programs. This paper focuses on teacher education, more specifically, on strategies for faculty development of teacher educators in order that they will become proficient in teaching teachers how to teach critical viewing skills to children. An attempt has been made to identify factors that promote effective faculty development and subsequent curricular change and instructional improvement as well as to point out some of the obstacles.

We know from both experience and research that curricular change is a slow process. The evidence clearly shows that, even when federal monies are available to implement change, often it does not "take root" (7, p. 12). This being the case, what generalizations can we make about strategies for introducing educational change through teacher education?

1. Faculty development programs for teacher educators are a prerequisite for significant changes in teacher education programs and are extremely important for effecting subsequent changes in elementary and secondary education programs.

2. There is a sizeable body of literature and research relating to the effects of television on the learning of children which has not been adequately disseminated to teacher educators and classroom teachers.

3. Teacher educators must develop an awareness of the need for changes in teacher education curricula in order for a faculty development program to be successful. Strategies must be devised, therefore, for teacher educators to become cognizant of the need to teach children critical television viewing skills.

4. A plan for incorporating the teaching of critical viewing skills into a teacher education program should be carefully developed to assure success. Basic to the planning process is the formulation of realistic goals and objectives for the project.

5. The involvement of faculty members in planning and conducting faculty development programs is essential for the success of the program. "Ownership" is a powerful intrinsic motivating force.

6. Firsthand experience as an observer of and as a participant in teaching critical viewing skills is conductive to changing teaching style.

7. Encouragement and support of the status leader(s) in a program of faculty development and curricular change are imperative for the complete institutionalization of the change. Administrative edict alone is ineffective. The dean's and departmental chairperson's roles are primarily that of providing moral support rather than "how-to-do-it" advice.

8. The difference between a successful project of curricular change and one that sooner or later fails depends primarily on the strategies used in implementing and maintaining the innovation and not on the availability of federal support monies.

In conclusion, the promotion of a curricular innovation to the institutional stage is a difficult undertaking. According to the *Randy Study*: (8) No simple or sure way can be found to effect educational change and have it persist. Nor is any single factor *the* answer to successful innovation, whether it be money, a new technique, or a change in personnel. Rather the fate of an innovation depends on the complex interplay among characteristics of the innovative project itself and the institutional setting it seeks to change.

Although I am not fully informed about the body of knowledge and skills related to children and television and the implications of those for education, it is my belief that it is an important area for curricular change and that much more should be done.

It seems to me that this conference will have a significant effect upon making curricular space for teaching critical receivership skills in both the nation's schools and its teacher education programs.

Footnotes

Fred H. Wood, Steven R. Thompson, and Frances Russell, "Designing Effective Staff Development Programs," chapter submitted for 1981 ASCD Yearbook.

Federal Programs Supporting Educational Change, prepared for the USOE, Dept. of HEW, by the Rand Corporation, April 1975, Vol. IV.

Milton E. Ploghoft and James A. Anderson, "Television Receivership Skills: The New Social Literacy," *The Social Science Record, Winter, 1977, pp. 8-13.*

Gene E. Hall, "Facilitating Institutional Change Using the Individual as the Frame of Reference," Teacher Education: *Renegotiating Roles for Mainstreaming,* editing by Judith K. Grosenick and Maynard C. Reynolds. Reston, VA: The Council for Exceptional Children, 1978, pp. 63-69.

Randy Study, op. cit., p. 9.

Ibid., p. 31.
Ibid., p. 12.

Ibid.

The Environment of Education Innovation:
Pitfalls and Pathways at the District and Local Level

Dr. Fritz Hess

The dynamics of local school districts are crucial to the success of innovative programming throughout the nation. No projects, however logical or appealing, will be workable unless they find acceptance at the local level.

Because of American education's diversity, no analysis can hope to include all the pitfalls and pathways to innovation at each district level. Yet a survey of local experiences can still be useful, and a detailed examination of the development of one system which has demonstrated particular success may point the way for other areas.

Pitfalls to Innovation in One District

The difficulties of innovation at the local level are numerous. Obviously, some systems, because of factors such as demographic makeup and political characteristics, are more open to change than are others. For a number of reasons, it is probably accurate to characterize the focus of this analysis, the East Syracuse-Minoa, New York, Central School District, as an organization which has confronted more than its share of pitfalls.

Like many of the so-called "central" school districts, East Syracuse-Minoa was put together from various small systems early in the 1960's. During the

---

Dr. Fritz Hess is Superintendent of Schools East Syracuse-Minoa Central Schools East Syracuse, New York 13057 half decade immediately following centralization, the component organizations still behaved in an autonomous fashion. Despite the existence of a central board and a central administration, curriculum and financial planning remained decentralized. Within the system, decision-making was basically vertical. Horizontal interaction was the exception. "Don't rock the boat" was the order of the day in the neighborhoods as well as in the schools.

The general inertia which marked the community and its educational system was the product of various influences. To a certain extent, it arose from the preference for the status quo which marks localities throughout the world. Whenever decision-making is reduced to the community level, inertia seems to increase. It is no accident that the House of Representatives, whose members come from district rather than statewide constituencies, is the more conservative of the two components of Congress.

A loss of public confidence in education during recent years has also hindered innovation within school districts. Originating in the failure of education to solve all of society's problems, this lack of faith has become symptomatic of a general disillusionment with public institutions. At East Syracuse, the impact of this pattern has been predictable. It has led to questioning of the efficacy of basic programming and has made the development of popular commitment to innovation an extremely difficult assignment.

Another general pitfall to innovation has been the financial climate of the late seventies. Resource constraints and inflation have limited basic programming in schools and other sectors of public affairs. The impact of this pattern has been twofold. From a direct standpoint, it has limited the number of dollars available for innovation from state, federal, and local sources. Indirectly, it has created a mood of retrenchment which discourages new programming.

Another general influence worthy of note has been the professional insecurity which premeates many school districts. At the local level, the status quo is frequently a comfortable alternative to innovation, especially when "rocking the boat" may endanger one's job. It is no secret that plenty of education degree holders are looking for employment.

From a general perspective, innovation can sometimes be an obstacle to innovation. This seeming paradox is explained by the fact that during the 1960's many new programs were implemented without planning or quality control. The result of this push toward change for the sake of change, in many areas, was the establishment of inferior curricula with eventual adverse public reaction.

These general patterns formed important barries to innovation at the local level. Yet various specific influences, especially local demographics, were also influential and constituted a significant pitfall to change. Communities which predated the centralized system and a network of socio-economic influences were two of these most important specific patterns.

Scattered across the nation, centralized school systems include a diverse spectrum of local communities: urban neighborhoods giving way to suburban developments which merge into rural villages. The conservative traditions in many of these areas has worked against challenges to the status quo. Pressure from local interest groups has had to be pre-empted before change could be implemented on a district-wide basis.

Together, the various general and specific influences noted above seem to block the course of innovation at the local level by encouraging the development of myths concerning change. No listing of these myths would be complete, yet a few are suggested here.

An extremely prevalent one is the notion that innovation is not really substantial programming, that it is just window dressing. Inherent in this view is the idea that most innovation in school districts is change for the sake of change, that new projects are instituted by bored teachers and administrators seeking to relieve their daily monotony and satisfy their egos.

Related to this idea is the myth that innovation inevitably conflicts with traditional educational methods. Upholders of this approach cling to the notion that "what was good enough for my generation is good enough for today's kids." They imply that because new programming may add to or modify an established curriculum, it must also violate the assumptions which underlie that core.

Another popular myth grew out of the injunction against "rocking the boat" in local districts. This approach categorizes all change as movement toward open classrooms. Its perpetrators claim that all innovation will inevitably bring disorder and disciplinary problems.

Yet another myth assumes that innovation must take the form of separate programming, segregated from the regular curriculum. It includes the notion that, in order to deal with modification of existing subject matter or instructional patterns, a district must divide its programming. In its most diluted form, the argument supports the establishment of separate classes in existing schools. In its most extreme application, the approach sees special buildings, outside present structures, as the logical foci for change.

This listing of myths suggests that rationalizations underline some opposition to change within school districts. The easy and convenient logic of these misconceptions traps not only the community and the media, but also, occasionally, teachers and administrators as well.

The range of these pitfalls to innovation suggests that the pathways which avoid them cannot be of a tentative or piecemeal nature. They must comprehensively address the future of education and the means of attaining it.

Pathways to Innovation in One District

The process of identifying pitfalls to innovation is somewhat easier than that of devising the means to overcome them. Analysis, however insightful and valuable, is less taxing than implementation.

At East Syracuse-Minoa, the road to innovation has been long and difficult. While the district has enjoyed considerable successes, it has also suffered from misfires. Following are a few general observations concerning the district's past efforts.

An essential precondition to any innovative movement is an administrative commitment to change. The superintendent employed by East Syracuse-Minoa from the late 1960's through the present time has maintained a consistent dedication to improving instruction and curricula in the system. Through wide ranging skills in program development, business management, and personnel allocation, the superintendent has been able to translate this dedication into results. Assembling a like-minded administrative staff has helped considerably.

Once a district becomes dedicated to change, it needs a comprehensive evaluation of its existing programming. East Syracuse-Minoa evaluated each existing instructional effort during the late 1960's. Applying various criteria, we ascertained our strengths and weaknesses of curricula and courses, both in isolation and as they related to the perceived general needs of the district.

Although desirable, recruitment of new staff is an option of limited value in most local districts. The agonizingly slow process of teacher turnover and the even slower process of principal turnover may require several years to evolve the critical nucleus necessary to make even small projects a reality. Under these conditions, recourse to staff inservice training becomes necessary.

Education of staff within the school system may take any number of forms, ranging from direct instruction to group-oriented sharing of experiences. Whatever the precise approach, the interests and energies of staff are directed to create the attitudes and use the resources necessary for change.

At East Syracuse-Minoa, inservice training has been instrumental in the creation of a climate favoring change, as well as in the implementation of various specific approaches. Enrichment, reading in content area, and gifted and talented programming would not have been possible without the recruiting and training which produced large-scale staff commitment in these areas. In each of these cases, it was important that inservice procedures be developed which could be carried out directly within short periods of time. Most effective were three day orientation workshops, summer study sessions, and periodic reinforcement sessions.

Beyond inservice training, successful innovation at the local level hinges on the ability to maintain staff involvement and commitment to programs. This process not only requires staff participation in the evolution of projects, but also efforts to keep staff appraised of progress and to recognize the staff's performance. Maintaining this involvement is an ongoing concern, and no easy approaches will suffice. At East Syracuse-Minoa, teachers who participate in the mathematics enrichment program, for instance, are kept informed of students' progress toward the project's objectives through inservice sessions and program bulletins. Teachers are also apprised of students' successes in related efforts, such as the county-wide mathematics symposium. Thus, the staff's role in producing significant change is recognized through these mechanisms and special messages.

In addition to staff's aid in innovation is the role of effective public relations. No project, however meaningful, will ever gain momentum unless it is publicized. Publicity increases staff and public knowledge of activities and builds a general climate conducive to innovation. Beyond these considerations, remember that local constituencies have a legal right to information concerning school activities. Educators would be remiss in their duties if they neglected to satisfy public desires.

At East Syracuse-Minoa, curricular innovation is publicized through various means. Not only do we deal with local media as already noted, but also the district has created its own medium, a monthly newsletter bringing verbal and visual pictures of new programs into each home. Parents Night and public orientation functions within the various schools also emphasize special approaches involving children. And at board of education meetings, curricular improvements are emphasized and supported at suitable times.

Beyond these specific components of innovation, it appears that various dynamic factors also shape pathways to change at the local level. One major influence, not suprisingly, is the success of existing efforts. The quicker new programming can produce measureable and demonstrable results, the more favorable will be the climate for further change.

In this context, it seems particularly important that initial innovative efforts within districts be approached with high probability of success. Although all projects should be undertaken with a commitment to excellence, it is particularly significant that extreme efforts be applied to first attempts. At East Syracuse-Minoa, Title I reading and other initial projects were implemented after we concluded that sufficient resources existed to produce success. Applying major efforts to developing of these programs produced a strong foundation for additional curricular improvement.

Once initial projects have achieved success, a momentum of innovation may evolve. Various forces may produce this pattern. The content of initial projects may directly suggest subsequent efforts. At East Syracuse-Minoa, enrichment programming for bright students spawned one of the state's first comprehensive efforts to meet the needs of gifted and talented students.

The openmindedness and challenge engendered by those first innovative moves may also support additional projects. Once staff and public eyes have been opened to the possibilities of innovation, the process can become a matter of local pride, a bandwagon which many may opt to join.

The momentum of successful programming may also contribute financial support to innovate. As money is appropriated for new efforts, it becomes part of the ongoing budgeting process. In subsequent years, amounts initially appropriated may be matched or added to, creating a reservoir of support for programming. The comprehensive curricular improvements being developed in reading, mathematics, and other areas have been made possible through the evolution of a structure of funding in these areas. In other instances, most notably the social sciences, stockpiling of financial resources has made possible the introduction of new approaches such as a television viewing skills curriculum.

One final point must clearly be emphasized. Evaluation is the critical keystone of the innovative arch, for it links attempts at change with established curricula. It analyzes developments to determine if they should become part of established patterns, and it points the way to improvement or suggests that further effort would not be wisely spent. At East Syracuse-Minoa, evaluation is continuously applied to present and potential programs, to recognize success and prescribe further change when it is needed.

From the foregoing discussion, the pitfalls to educational change at the district level are obvious. At the same time, however, pathways around these obstacles clearly exist. Remember, though, that the suggestions offered here are only of a general nature. Each school system possesses its own versions of these obstacles, and each must find its own means of circumnavigating them. In the last analysis, each district must adapt the above suggestions as needed to pioneer its own pathways to change.

The essential force seems to be the administrative dedication which makes the process possible. A total commitment on the part of key leadership personnel is the ingredient which enables a system to progress, no matter what the obstacles.

SECTION VI

The Intended Effects of Critical Viewing Curricula

The three speakers who appeared on the final day of the conference represented remarkably different points of view. Banks provided a workman review of the preliminary studies concerning child development and media understanding. Writing from an industry perspective, he counseled patience in looking for information-rich advertising. At the same time he predicted its ultimate arrival as viewer skills and advertiser understanding of those skills increase.

Lull spoke from his own tightly drawn perspective of what ought to be. He saw great dangers in television—"An Illness," he called it. Receivership skills is more than a bit like blaming the victim for the crime, in his view. The real solution is in the reduction of the all too potent bigness of advertising, business and media. Lull provided an interesting contrast from the up-beat, we-can-do-it attitudes of most of the conferees.

Gerbner maintained his position as an eminent theoretician of the mass media. He saw television as a unifying force returning us to the cultural integration of oral societies. Television is common to all, a repository of all that is basic in values, goals and aspirations. It bridges the breaches in our society of industrial specialization, economic class, and educational elitism. Receivership skills, for Gerbner, is part of the liberal arts with studies in areas like receivership skills providing the advantage of choice and the ability to select from culture those elements suitable to an individual's purposes.

The Effects of Critical Viewing Skills Curriculum on Advertising Forms and Strategies

Seymour Banks

INTRODUCTION

Almost a year and a half ago, I gave a paper at an Airlie Conference urging the development of consumer education curricula for elementary school children, with media literacy as a prime topic. That concept was formulated on the basis of my awareness of several developments already underway in various areas dealing with children's ability to cope with television—the development and testing of critical viewing curricula or teaching units, the evaluation of the consequence of co-viewing television by children and significant "others"; and experiments in classroom exposure to and discussion of commercials. I am delighted those developments are continuing and that I have been asked to participate in this conference as an advertising professional—however, everyone must be aware of the fact that my company affiliation is for identification and not for attribution. It is my personal point of view that the development of critical viewing skills will have only beneficial effects both for children and the advertising community.

Having given you my conclusion - that the development of critical viewing skills is beneficial - I will work my way to it in three steps. The first part of my talk will be a summary of research studies on attempts to use classroom

---

Seymour Banks, Ph.D., is Vice President of Research for Leo Burnett U.S.A.

exercises to acquaint children with the functional intent of television commercials. Next I will review some other relevant research dealing with children's information-processing capabilities. Finally, I will discuss the implication of these two bodies of research for advertising.

TEACHING CHILDREN TO COPE WITH COMMERCIALS

Research on formal classroom means of acquainting children with the functional intent and techniques of television commercials is another example of a good idea whose time had come, with much of the ferment arising out of the discussions on children's television programs and commercials at both the Federal Trade Commission and the Federal Communications Commission during the early and mid 70's. *Zeitgeist* is a good explanation for such simultaneous effort, including unsponsored work at the Institute of Communication Research at Stanford, two grants by the National Science Foundation: one to a Harvard/Minnesota coalition, the other to a UCLA team; and an East Coast effort sponsored by the National Association of Broadcasters. However, an insider's view suggests that the comfortable bar and lounge at Airlie House had much to do with this development also. My bibliography of this American *samizdhat* literature is appended.

As might be expected from a situation in which different researchers respond independently to the *Zeitgeist,* there are both similarities and differences in their work. The populations of children studied range in age from kindergartners to 8th grade. Also, the various researchers had different purposes in mind when they brought children face to face with television commercials in classrooms - efforts ranged from finding means of facilitating effective consumer behavior by young children to finding means to immunize them against commercial appeals (3, 4, 7, 12, and 16).

The most important conclusion that one can draw from these studies is that they all worked [1] by working, I mean that, at the very least, satisfactory proportions of the children tested became aware of the factors, both physical and functional, which differentiate commercials from programs. In addition, the experimental data indicated that children evaluated commercials in a much more sophisticated manner than they had done previously. In many ways, the most remarkable finding of this work is that not much work was required to accomplish these results: the classroom training sessions used by these researchers were quite brief - two studies used

---

[1] The UCLA project under the direction of Professors Seymour and Norma Feshbach is no more than half-way along so their findings are extremely tentative; the strongest that can be said is that their training conditions produce predictable changes among second and fourth graders. Little effect appears among kindergartners so far but special pre-school material may be tried among this group.

a single instructional session; the longest consumed 3 1/2 hours spread over nine days. Incidentally, Wackman, Wartella and Ward (16) who conducted the last mentioned study at Minnesota with kindergartners reported that, "there was reasonably substantial impact on children's understanding of persuasive intent (of commercials) eight months after training."

Although concern was directed to acquainting pre-schoolers with basic marketplace concepts rather than with commercials, per se, an effort at the University of Wisconsin merits attention. Again, the amount of training was relatively small - three instructional units spread over a two week period. As with the work on commercials per se; the children responded positively to the training (14).

The conclusion to be drawn from this body of work, in my opinion, goes beyond the demonstration that young children possess television "readiness" to borrow a nursery school/kindergarten term. It also has theoretical impact on theories of child development, both supporting the learning theory approach and challenging a crude Piagetian cognitive deficiency concept. It is interesting to find parallel statements between Gelman in her 1978 review of the cognitive development literature "the case can now be made that the preschooler's cognitive capacities have been underestimated" (5, see also 2, 6 and 13), and the comments made by Wackman, Ward and Wartella after their consumer education efforts with kindergartners "Our findings suggest that kindergarten children know more about commercials and they retain and use more information from commercials than we thought previously... Overall, it would appear that we—and other researchers—have underestimated kindergartners' capabilities" (16, pp. 139-140).

CHILDREN: ACTIVE OR PASSIVE PROCESSORS OF TELEVISION

To many critics, the best description of children and television may be found in an old ACT recruiting film which showed children staring at a set so mesmerized they couldn't move, so exhausted their eyes kept blinking open and closed; or in the title of a fairly recent book: (TV) The Plug-In Drug (18).

However, there are three research efforts which give quite a different view of the child's performance vis-a-vis television. The starting point is research on attention. An excellent review of this literature starts with infants and points out that as they became familiar with their world, they attend systematically (hence selectively) to it. As children develop, their search activity for information improves in efficiency as indicated by the ratio of attention paid to relevant versus irrelevant information. The authors conclude that the fact that there is such demonstrable selectivity in a child's interaction to his environment idicates that the child is always an active seeker after information (11).

The next research effort I shall discuss reflects a return to the uses and gratifications approach that characterized television research in the late 50's and early 60's in the sense that they deal with the interaction between the child and the medium. In a series of studies on the formal features of television - pacing, level of action, amount of variability, camera techniques like cuts and zooms and auditory techniques such as music and special effects Aletha Huston-Stein, John Wright and their colleagues at the University of Kansas have found that both age-related cognitive development and experience with the television medium increases the child's ability to use and understand the codes of the medium (8 and 17). But more applicable to our discussion is their pointing out that because a television viewer seems behaviorally passive while processing television information, there's a strong skepticism about children's ability to process televised information.

Nevertheless, children beginning at the age of 2 or 3 develop the ability to decode what is happening on the screen by constructing and revising a cognitive model of the situation. The developmental progression is seen as moving from exploration of television guided by stimulus salience toward systematic and logical search guided by internally mediated considerations of relevance and informativeness (19).

Finally, only two months ago, Prof. Daniel Anderson reported that his work has led him to change his original view of children's television viewing from being a passive, stimulus-bound activity to one involving an active transaction between the child, the television set and the TV viewing environment. He has discovered that young children's understanding of television is a major determinant of their visual attention. Thus, his conception of young children's TV viewing is as a cognitively active learned behavior sensibly intermixed with relatively passive unlearned cognitive processes, representative of the active, growing and selective cognitive activity that the child brings to many everyday situations (1).

IMPLICATIONS FOR TELEVISION ADVERTISING

Both the work on classroom consumer education about television commercials and the information processing approach to television viewing lead to a view of children as an active processor of televised material. In addition, although we don't want to claim adult-like competence for children, it is clear that the most recent era of research indicates that their cognitive capacities have been underestimated and that they have substantial learning capabilities. However one of the keys to this new era is a clear understanding that research with children has been riddled by the experimenter effect: the language which comes naturally to researchers has bewitched, bothered and bewildered their child subjects (15).

As Gelman put it, the researcher must make it possible for the child to understand the rules of the experimenter's game (5). Mischel has found that by the time children reach the age of 10, they have accumulated an impressive ability to predict the outcome of classical experimental and social psychology; however this ability was revealed only when those experiments were carefully described in detail, stripped of jargon and phrased in age-appropriate ways (10).

I see this double awareness of children's fairly substantial cognitive capacities and highly setting - and language - bound responses as having the capability of leading to more information-rich advertising but only if it uses forms of communication and language more specifically adapted to a child's linguistic or semantic capacities. The prototype of this development can be found in a research project sponsored by the Children's Advertising Review Unit, National Advertising Division, Council of Better Business Bureaus to investigate the effectiveness of the language used in children's commercials to divulge necessary information - these are known in the trade as disclaimers. It was found that the disclaimer Assembly Required, apparently written by lawyers, was not understood well even by children in the upper elementary grades; however the phrase "You have to put it together" was almost universally understood (9).

One should not expect overnight changes in children's advertising, especially in response to material which is still so new that it exists only in the form of academic research reports or papers at conferences. Nevertheless, there are communication gatekeepers in the advertising community who bring such literature and their findings to their colleagues. It is difficult for enthusiasts to wait for such an apparently uncertain evolutionary process but I recommend patience. This recommendation comes naturally from some one like me who combines strong professional interests in research on children's understanding of and response to commercials with an absolute rejection of the mandating of research.

References

1. Anderson, D.R. Active and passive processes in children's television viewing. Paper presented at the American Psychological Association Convention, New York, 1979.

2. Donaldson, M. The mismatch between school and children's minds. *Human Nature,* 1979, 60-67.

3. Donohue, T.R., Meyer, T.P. and Henke, L.L. Learning about television commercials: The impact of instructional units on children's perceptions of motives and intent. Unpublished manuscript, National Association of Broadcasters, 1978.

4. Feshbach, S. Increasing children's understanding of television commercials. Personal correspondence, October 5, 1979.

5. Gelman, R. Cognitive development. *Annual Reviews of Psychology, 29,* 1978, 297-332.

6. Ginsburg, H. and Doslowski, B. Cognitive development. *Annual Reviews of Psychology,* 27, 1976, 29-61.

7. Henke, L., Donohue, T.R. and Meyer, T.P. Learning about TV commercials: Effects of an instructional unit on black children's perceptions of commercial intent and credibility. Unpublished manuscript, University of Hartford, no date.

8. Huston-Stein, A. Television and growing up: The medium gets equal time. Paper presented to the American Psychological Association convention, San Francisco, 1977.

9. Liebert, R.M., Liebert, D.E. and others. Effects of television commercial disclaimers on the product expectations of children. Unpublished manuscript, Brookdale International Institute, 1976.

10. Mischel, W. On the interface of cognition and personality: Beyond the person-situation debate. *American Psychologist, 34* 1979, 740-54.

11. Pick, A.D., Hess, V.L. and Frankel, D.G. *Childrens attention: The development of selectivity.* Chicago: The University of Chicago Press, 1975.

12. Roberts, D.I., Gibson, W. and others. Immunizing children against commercial appeals. Paper presented to the American Psychological Association convention, Toronto, 1978.

13. Siegal, L. and Brainerd, C.J. (Eds.). *Alternatives to Piaget: Critical essays on the theory.* New York: Academic Press, 1978.

14. Stampfl, R.W., Moschis, G. and Lawton, J.T. Consumer education and the pre-school child. *Journal of Consumer Affairs, 12,* 1978, 12-29.

15. Stevenson, H.W. Television and the behavior of preschool children. *Television and social behavior, 2,* 346-371, Rubinstein, E.A. and Comstock, G.A. eds., Washington, D.C.: U.S. Government Printing Office, 1972.

16. Wackman, D.B., Ward, S. and Wartella, E. Children's information processing of television advertising. Final report to the National Science Foundation on grant No. APR76-20770.

17. Watkins, B.A., Huston-Stein, A., Wright, J.C. and others. Attention to television programs varying in action and pace by children at two age levels. Department of Human Development, University of Kansas, research report No. 6, no date.

18. Winn, M. *The plug-in drug.* New York: Viking Press, 1977.

19. Wright, J.C., Watkins, B.A. and Huston-Stein, A. Active vs. passive television viewing: A model of the development of television information processing by children. Department of Human Development, University of Kansas, no date.

Social Uses of Television in Family Settings
And A Critique of Receivership Skills

James Lull

INTRODUCTION

I'm going to comment on two major areas—the first of which will concern television's role in family communications, the second is a critique of the receivership skills curriculum and some of the matters with which we have dealt during this conference. I come to this conference as a communication researcher who is primarily interested in families rather than as an educator who has had experience or a particular interest in receivership skills or other alternative curricular approaches. In fact, the term "receivership skills" is something rather new to me and a concept about which I have learned quite a lot here during the past few days.

James Lull is Assistant Professor in The Department of Speech at the University of California at Santa Barbara.

TELEVISION VIEWING IN FAMILY SETTINGS

I use the ethnographic method in order to study families and home life. It's a data-gathering technique which allows us to learn a variety of things about human communication that other methods of social science have not permitted. We are able to examine carefully how families process communication and, particularly, what they do with messages that come into their homes from the mass media. I don't think it's possible to study the intricacies and the subtleties ot those behaviors very well with experimental or social survey research approaches. The ethnographic method, where the researcher lives in with families and studies them at first-hand, reveals in great detail who the family members are and what they're about. By observing families' naturally-grounded behaviors, their attitudes and observable actions, the processes of family communication become apparent.

Families are micro-social units that can be studied as interdependent entities which ongoingly communicate in order to construct social reality in the natural habitat of the home. These interdependent parts can be examined in relation to each other—parents to children, children to children, parents to parents. The fundamental question I raise is how does television play a role in the ways that families construct their interpersonal realities?

Most of this conference has been oriented toward television program content. We have talked about content in a variety of ways. For instance, we discussed how children cognitively process various kinds of content—program themes, instructional materials, advertising messages—at various stages within their psychological development. There has been some excellent research reported here. We have looked at programs which have been created by alternative production sources. We have talked about the content of those programs and how they have been received by children. We have heard terms discussed in relation to instructional approaches such as "analysis, evaluation and expression" of ideas about meaning which inheres within the program content of television.

But we know from our own experience that the social consumption of media is not, in reality, limited by the constraints of content. To me, media literacy, or any contemporary curriculum that examines television, must also regard seriously non-content aspects of the viewing experience. The ways in which media structure our lives, alter our lives, the ways in which we use media to construct our interpersonal relationships can also be analyzed and evaluated systematically. The pervasiveness of television makes sensitivity to these issues crucial. The set is likely to be turned on, not turned off, in most homes. You don't turn the set on anymore, you turn the set off...that's the decision, NOT to watch. It's already on, it's assumed that it will be on. The act is to turn it off.

During the past four or five years, my students and I have lived with more than 200 families for periods of three to seven days each. Data collected during this time have permitted the development of a typology whereby the features of certain social implications of television that are not entirely content-bound are organized and presented. Many of these activities are not immediately obvious behaviors but they play powerful roles in family communication. I would like to call your attention to some specifics in the typology and I would ask that those educators who are interested in curriculum development with an accent on media might think in terms of broadening the scope of what we have talked about here during the past few days to at least include the spirit of some of the things which I will discuss. Some of the points I will make will perhaps resonate with your own experience, the experience of your students, perhaps with your own children, or with the families where you grew up.

The typology of the social uses of television is organized into two major components: Structural and relational uses—how the family structures home life and how we relate to one another in the presence of the media. The structural component has two subsets. One is *environmental,* meaning that we live in a media environment, the television environment, which as I have pointed out is taken for granted in most families. This factor is characterized by activities such as turning the television on for background noise, for companionship, and that we use it as a convenient source of constant entertainment in order to relax, to laugh, to emote. It also has a *regulative* function, in the sense that it regulates the ways in which we punctuate time. For instance, families know that, "it's really eight o'clock, because Show X is on the air." That's also the time when the kids really must go to bed. Talk patterns: Don't talk to dad while his favorite show is on."

But, it's the relational aspects of television's place in the social world that interest me the most. These uses of the medium are even more subtle, and they don't always occur in the presence of the television set. The social reality that television helps us construct in the home is not limited to the moments which we call the viewing experience. A simple, but powerful, example is the agenda-setting function of television where, in the first place, we might talk about what is on television as we watch. The set immediately directs our attention to particular program themes or ideas. But we also know that television provides the opportunity for us to set conversational agendas after viewing. All of you know that children come to school fully prepared to talk about what they saw on television the night before. It dominates their interaction at school. As children relate to each other during play, they talk about the television characters. There is a conversational agenda being set apart from the viewing experience.

FOUR COMPONENTS OF SOCIAL USE

There are four components of the relational aspect of the social uses of television typology. These are communication facilitation, affiliation/-avoidance, social learning, and competence/dominance. Now, I'll try to illustrate what is meant by these constructs. In order to *facilitate communication,* a child, or an adult, can use television to illustrate their experiences. For instance, a child who is trying desperately to tell his mother about a fight that happened at school, and, not being able to find the right words to describe it on its own terms, says something like, "Oh, you know mom, it's like on the Brady Bunch. They were all kicking and fighting with each other." Mom understands. What are the implications of that kind of interaction? The child has used television as the primary referent for the parent to understand a real-world event. We have been talking during this conference about how television programs are very special constructed social realities themselves. We know that certain corporate values and bureaucratic mandates will dictate the themes and story lines which television presents. So, when a child refers to a television example in order to explain a real-world experience, perhaps that fact should be pointed out to the child. The parent might intervene at this point and say to the child, "Wait a minute, let's stop." If the parent is trained to do so, he or she can use this moment to educate the child about a particular way in which television is affecting the child.

Children also use television examples in order to enter adult conversations because children know that television's agenda is cross-generational common ground. Television is also used in some homes to reduce anxiety. You don't have to look at each other while the TV is on. This applies not only to family members, but also when guests arrive television is often used to reduce the discomfort of being in the close proximity of someone outside the family. Individuals who are watching may differ greatly but probably share histories of the program as well as the opportunity to cooperatively interpret what they view together.

The second component of the typology is *affiliation/avoidance.* It refers to the use of television as a means for facilitating physical and verbal contact or neglect. In one of my studies, a married couple with whom I lived touched each other only twice during the week-long observation period. Both times they used a medium to focus their attention. In one case, their little girl came home from school and, after dinner, she told a story about something that had happened during school. During the story, dad took mom and put her on his lap while they listened to her. The only other time that they touched each other at least in the nonbedroom aspect of their homelife (there are limits to ethnography) was when television was on. The husband was asleep on the couch and his wife, sitting on the floor, snuggled up next to his bare feet which were resting on the lower part of his comfortable chair. They shared a moment of physical "intimacy" while watching the set.

Some of the typical uses and gratifications research in communication points to the use of television in order to create family harmony—people at home sharing the viewing experience, creating a consensual emotional response to the program, predicting together what they think the conclusion to the show might be. Here's another opportunity for an educational application, by the way. While television is a resource for sharing verbal, intellectual, and emotional responses, families could be reminded that the materials with which they work, the resources generated by television programming, are imported to them and are laden with values.

Television allows for conflict reduction. If people are angry with each other, they don't have to argue so long as the television set is on. It's a convenient distraction. Television may contribute to maintenance of interpersonal relationships at home by providing vicarious avenues for participation in emotional or professional worlds not available to those at home. In one study I conducted a woman insisted upon watching all the medical shows. She had wanted to be a nurse, but never achieved that goal in the real world. Her husband encouraged her to watch medical shows because, if she watched these programs, thereby participating in the world of medicine through television, she was able to become a nurse for those hours. This made the limits that their marriage provided more bearable for her. He recognized this and encouraged her to view.

Social learning is the third construct of this portion of the typology. We all know that we learn a lot from television. It creates and directs our consumer and political choices. We model our behavior based, in part, upon the action of the television's characters. Roles are imitated. Families learn how to carry out various roles by viewing television's families. The Waltons, in particular, has provided role models for how to be in the virtuous family. Some people say they consciously watch television in order to learn how to behave in certain roles.

Communication researchers have discovered media's usefulness for problem solving. We saw evidence of this from the early studies of the radio soap operas. They demonstrated how social implications arise from the fact that people learn how to deal interpersonally with their problems from radio's examples. This is a body of academic research that is not well known by educators at the secondary and elementary levels, but is potentially very useful to them. Why can't these sources of information be incorporated into the receivership skills curriculum? Value transmission—how people find out and transmit to each other what is right, what is true, what works—is another relational use of television. The notion of television confirming status—let's call this to people's attention.

Competence/dominance is the final construct of concern here. In order to enact their roles, mothers and fathers sometimes use television as a way to demonstrate competency as a parent. The parent can use television to regulate the children's behavior by not allowing them to watch certain shows. A byproduct of this is that the mother or father has used television as a resource for demonstrating parental competency. Role reinforcement—a father or mother watching television with the children sees something in a program that reflects and reinforces a similar situation at home. Television also provides substitute role portrayals for single parent families. Television provides opportunities for exercising authority, for validating knowledge, and to promote argumentation when desired. Television can be used as a resource to argue out loud, aggressively—even with hostility. It can also be used very subtly. For instance, in one family where I lived, a man and woman watched television together and saw a couple on television who were embracing and kissing. It was very romantic, very sensual scene. The man at home, never taking his eyes off the set, mumbled to his wife, "Are these two married?" His wife, also never taking her eyes off the set, said, "Do they look married to you?" She implied, "Of course they're not married. Married people don't embrace like that. And, you haven't touched me like that in a long time."

People do not automatically or homogeneously use television for the purposes which have been discussed. In a recent study 85 trained observers were placed in homes for the same three-day period. We found that families which have different interpersonal communication styles use television differently socially. There are socio-oriented families that stress harmonious relationships where individuals don't challenge each other's authority. In concept-oriented families, on the other hand, family members are taught to challenge each others beliefs verbally—they argue and debate issues. We have found that the social uses of television are employed differentially by families with contrasting communicative styles. Families which contain members most likely to use television for the purposes which I have described today are the socio-oriented groups.

OBSERVATIONS ON RECEIVERSHIP SKILLS

Now, I'd like to make some observations about the value and potential effect of the receivership skills curricula, particularly as it potentially affects families. It's difficult to predict the nature of family life in a dynamic society. We know, for instance, that family members say they watch television more now than ever before, but they like it less. So regardless of what family members tell us, their spoken attitudes may not predict their media behavior. Who knows, by 1985 they may say that they absolutely hate television but watch it 20 hours a day. But I do know that by means of consciousness-raising efforts involving families and conducted through school systems, nursery schools, PTA organizations, and other clubs and organizations that are interested, you can certainly discuss meaningfully the issues that have been raised during this conference. Families are very interested in all of this. A major problem, however, is that most of these formal organizations are composed only of middle-class families and upperclass families.

Television As An Illness

Let me get to the point of the critique. I believe that television is an illness in society. In treating another social illness, alcoholism, recovery is most likely to occur when the illness is regarded as an organic problem. All components of the organism must be treated. If there is an alcoholic family member, for instance, the best therapy is to bring the entire family into a recuperative setting and show them that the alcoholic's problem does not exist in isolation—it is an illness which is accelerated through insensitive interaction. All aspects of the problem must be treated or the illness will not reside. I doubt that we would all be at this conference if we didn't agree that television is a social problem, an illness. The television problem, therefore, must also be treated organically. We have to think of it as a problem that involves the advertising industry, the broadcasting business, educational institutions, families, big business. First and foremost it involves big business because, ultimately, business controls the remainder of the organism.

In a sense, the receivership skills approach makes it look like we—educators and audience members—are the ones who ought to be responsible for remedying the problem. In many ways this conference has therefore perpetuated the status quo of poor television. Certainly all of us must deal with television as individuals, family members, and educators. But we're not going to see any major changes, any primary positive results, until the problems with broadcasting are treated organically whereby all components in the system are equally sensitive to and responsible for solving its difficulties. Why don't we have a sendership skills conference? The broadcast industry only does this in a very token way and it's handled by them as a public relations problem.

Television Can Use Us

I applaud the sensitivity that members of this conference have had to the fact that the mass media affect us individually and as a society. But some researchers continue to promote the idea that television is "used" by people—television doesn't do things to people. I don't buy that perspective for one second. We use television in various ways and television uses us. It's a transaction. The television viewing experience means that we obtain something—we can escape for awhile, we can be entertained, we can use it to construct our interpersonal realities at home, but ultimately what is happening is that broad and powerful patterns of political awareness and consumption are being created by the power structure that controls what is on television. This takes place not only through advertising, but in the selection of news stories, program themes, and so on.

"Receivership skills"—the name of it makes me nervous. It sounds too much like "good citizenship." We're told, "Be a good little receiver and a good little citizen. It's up to us as good little citizens to deal with the problems of television, to amplify the positive aspects of television, to make television viewing more meaningful, more pleasant, more instructive." These are some of the themes which come out of this conference and they bother me.

There is much more to the story. The case of Bayer Aspirin is a good example of how television affects us. More than 50% of over 300 people I have interviewed recently claim that Bayer is their preferred aspirin product. Bayer is five-grain aspirin just like any other aspirin product on the market. Why do more than 50% of the people who have a preference for an aspirin product say, "Bayer Aspirin?" The media don't affect us? If this is true, Bayer would not be named by so many aspirin consumers. The difference in aspirin sales is primarily attributable to Sterling Drugs' advertising of Bayer so regularly and for so many years. There are dozens and dozens of other examples that make the same point.

Receivership Skills Must Demystify Television

Any meaningful analysis of television as part of a school curriculum should not only demystify the technology of the medium but also demystify the economic structure of television. We know that we can effectively demystify the technical aspects of the medium. We can do so by going to a television studio to see what it's really like to produce a television program. We can show children that television programs are a constructed reality accomplished with special effects, characterizations, predictable story lines, and other techniques. Audience members' feelings toward television are structured differently after going through this experience. It's truly a consciousness—raising activity. But it's only one dimension of what could be done. The other crucial dimension is to examine very carefully the ways in which particular self-selecting, powerful institutions in this country control the agenda of television and, given the economic structure that we have, severely limit the opportunities for meaningful social change. In the receivership skills curriculum of the future, let's look carefully at how decisions are made in the television business, what the motivations are that direct the decisions that are made and the programs which result. Let's help children analyze the interdependence of the big institutions in this country—big advertising, big business, big media. Let's talk to them about how selected markets are created through the process of advertising. Let them know that there are only certain corporate institutions which are able to buy time on the airways, particularly during prime time.

CONCLUSION

The fact that we have mass media in place which inhibit the full flowering of discussions which could be generated about political and economic matters is a serious flaw in a democratic society. Nonetheless, as educators there are things we can do. First, we can teach the content and noncontent influences on media consumption referred to in the social uses of television typology which I have briefly outlined. Second, we can direct our attention not only to the demystification of the television technology, but to the demystification of the economic structure that governs mass communication in the United States. These are areas that are essentially neglected in media education so far and promise to enrichen the "receivership skills" curriculum as it is presently conceptualized.

Education For The Age of Television

George Gerbner

INTRODUCTION

I'd like to share with you my sense of the historic nature of this occasion. I think you are in the vanguard of the age in which we live, which, for purposes of our discussion, I shall call the age of television.

I begin with a kind of communication historical framework that is based on the assumption that people don't experience reality directly. We experience reality in a symbolic context that gives meaning to whatever we encounter. That symbolic context is sometimes called education, sometimes information, sometimes entertainment; I would like to call it storytelling.

We spend much of our lives learning stories, telling stories and communing through stories. Stories are told in many codes and in many modes. Sometimes they're called fairy tales, sometimes they're called science, sometimes they're called history.

We are born into an environment of stories. Much of our education consists of being told and learning how to tell stories. It is to the image of these stories that we construct a great fantasy—which is the fantasy of what the world is like, what we are like, who we are, and what is the past and perhaps the future. By fantasy, I don't mean that it's false but that it's purposive and synthetic.

George Gerbner is Professor and Dean, The Annenberg School of Communications, University of Pennsylvania.

THE STORIES OF LIVING

There are basically three kinds of stories.

First are the stories that show *how things work*. These are perhaps the most important. These are the stories that make visible the most important, therefore, invisible connections in life. By embodying them in people acting in situations coming to grips with certain difficulties and problems and either succeeding or failing, they make visible those invisible connections—the dynamics, the inner dynamics we must understand to have some notion of how things work. These stories are called drama and fiction and myth. Only they can invent the facts so as to lend themselves to the development of an insight into how things really work.

The second kind of story, is a story of *what things are*. These are stories that are high on what we might call facticity—the bits that correspond to some independently observable event we call a fact. They carry little information except when they are placed in a framework created by the first kind of storytelling of how things work. Then, they fill out this framework and give it a sense of verisimilitude and give it a sense of applicability. They show not only how things work but what these things are, and they give specific examples of the rules and the exceptions to the rules. These are stories called legend, today's news, that perform, very selectively, the function of telling us what things *are*.

The third kind of story is one of *value and of choice*. As if to say: if this is how things work, and if this is what things are, well then, what are we going to do about it? What are the choices and the values assigned to these choices? How are they weighed—on some scale of desirability, attractiveness, power? What are the styles of life that provide these choices, and what are the things that belong to these styles of life? At what price? These are stories that today we call mostly advertisements or commercials. Each one embodies a style of life into which certain things we call products, services, ideas, sometimes candidates, fit.

CULTURES AND STORIES

Now, all cultures have always told all three kinds of stories. You can't have a viable society and a fully acculturated and socialized human being without having lived with a set of these stories for many years and without having them integrated into a fantasy—much of it true, much of it inventive, all of it functional. That creates our notions of how things work, what things are, and what are the choices that we confront.

Pre-Industrial Cultural Stories

Each culture has woven together these stories in somewhat different ways. In pre-industrial, pre-print society, the stories were woven together in certain specific ways that we can call *ritualistic* because we couldn't say, "I don't have to know it, I don't have to remember it, I can look it up." There was no place to look it up. You did have to know it, you did have to remember, all that you really needed. And a pre-literate society therefore demands more of a human being in terms of capacity of stories and of inner resources than a modern society. Pre-literate people all over the world are tremendously resourceful because they must carry within themselves all of the stories and the application of these stories that they really need. And the way to do that is to learn them ritualistically.

These stories are also highly *institutionalized* in a pre-industrial, pre-print era. They are not invented by individuals who are specialists who write stories—they are part of the tradition into which children are born and in which they grow up to be accomplished storytellers, usually through the teachings of the parents and the family and the chiefs, the heads of the tribe or the community.

So, these stories are *total* in two ways. They belong to a total, organically composed repertory of stories, and secondly, they involve the total community. There are no great differences of style, taste, age, sex. Everyone gets introduced into the world of stories appropriate to a particular group at about the same time.

Next, they are all what we today would call *entertaining* which means they are compelling, they are inherently rewarding for their own sake. They cultivate a sense of rightness, a sense of place, a sense of belonging, a sense of selfhood which is what entertainment basically does. And because most of them are not specialized, they don't say, "You're not a mathematician so you don't like this kind of story we call math;" "you're not a scientist and you don't want the kind of story we call science," or "you're not a lawyer, therefore you don't need the kind of story we call law." The stories of a pre-print society are non-specialized stories; they are the mythology of the total community, which provide a sense of coherence and a belonging and which entertain the basic tenets, the basic values and the basic directions and meanings of the culture.

And finally, they are what today we will call the *socializing* process of the tribe or the community. It is these stories through which a new member becomes a member of the community in the full sense—takes on a role, takes on an understanding of place and development.

Industrial Cultures and Stories

We have an abrupt shift of scene with the industrial revolution. The first industrial machine is the printing press. The first industrial product is the book. The book is not only the first product, but a pre-requisite for all that is to follow including the breaking up of the ritual, of the organic collectiveness of the tribe and the community; the packaging of knowledge into capsules that can be sent, often smuggled over previously impenetrable boundaries; the breaking up of the unity of the community and its sense of belonging and meaning into different classes, different specialized crafts, over large regions and regional groups; the creation of what we now call different religious, and, of course, of public education and a literate print-based elite.

With the coming of industrialization, there are conflicting and competing classes, there are conflicting and competing specialized interests. Each of these competing interest groups and classes fights for the right to produce stories from its own points of view and to cultivate its own sense of belonging and of interest within the same larger community. These rights are guaranteed in the First Amendment.

The ritual is gone, the institutionalization of storytelling disappears with the abolition of licensing printers. The totality disappears because now instead of total organically-connected storytelling, we have various groups producing stories—all kinds of stories and all three types of stories pretty much from their own points of view.

The entirely compelling and entertaining function of all stories also disappears because specialization comes in. Each of the vocations, arts, crafts, sciences, statecraft and so on requires specialized storytelling, so it's no longer for everyone.

And what is for everyone and what is compelling to everyone is relegated to that section that we call entertainment—which is still the most important because it provides the common basis, the common myths by which we live.

And, finally, the socialization process—also breaks into many components. The family has its own role, the church has its own role, the school has its own role, the peer groups have their own role, the library, the government, the various media of communication all have a part in the total process of socialization. There is no longer a kind of unified process and control as existed for many, many thousands of years.

TELEVISION: THE NEW OLD CULTURE

We are describing the last two or three hundred years coming not to an end, but to another major transformation about thirty or forty years ago. The coming of television represents not an abrupt break but a transformation in the cultural situation in which we live and in which we tell all the stories. It does not supplant, but it is superimposed on the print culture with all its plurality and relative diversity, and it has certain rather specific, interesting, and, to us now, somewhat familiar characteristics.

First of all, television is a *ritual*. It is not like books or even like films. It is not selective—most people do not pick and choose by the program but by the clock, by the time of day, by the day of the week, by the week of the month, and the season of the year. It is a daily, weekly, and seasonal rhythm in which, by and large, the vast majority of the viewing public is non-selectively and ritualistically engaged.

Secondly, it is highly *institutionalized*. Unlike print, you have to get a license to get on the air. There are only a limited number of licenses available. So it has become an institutionalized and essentially centralized authoritatively granted privilege.

Next, it is again *total*. There is one basic formula to which the vast majority of programs, regardless of what you call them, have to adjust. The formula is called Cost-Per-Thousand. That means that the rating of a program divided by the cost of the program gives you the formula of what goes and what doesn't go. In other words, the cheapest, least objectionable programming. It has been found that viewers are really ritualized into the television habit; reducing the cost, putting the ritual on the assembly line is a natural tendency in the industry.

So you have again a total, organically composed programming concept for the total community. Parochialism, provincialism do not exist anymore. For all practical purposes, the persons living in the penthouse and in the ghetto watch much of the same cultural fare. One of the great attractions of television, especially for poor people, is that they can have a bond which they never had before—a very intimate bond with the rich and the famous and the powerful and all the celebrities and the power figures of their society.

Because of these compelling reasons, television is also all *entertainment*. It is all based on an entertainment formula in the sense that it is compelling, that it is for all, that it is not highly specialized, and that it entertains the basic beliefs of a society of which it is the chief cultural arm.

And finally, therefore, it is the central, by no means only, but the central most pervasive, most universal and only common *socializing* process of our community. It has taken the major part of, and therefore must have a major responsibility for, the acculturation of our children, the bringing of them into that mainstream of the common culture in which they develop much of their sense of what the standards are by which to judge oneself, one's parents, one's leaders, one's society and one's world.

In that sense, the age of television has no historic predecessor. The other media are used very differently and selectively. They require literacy, going out, and paying a certain amount of money per film, per book, or per magazine. If television has a historic predecessor at all, it is pre-industrial tribal religion. Only that had these features and characteristics.

And this brings us to the critical task of education in the age of television. I think that task is to build a fresh approach to the liberal arts.

I define the liberal arts as those skills and concepts that liberate the individual from an unquestioning dependence on the local and immediate culture environment. Until now it was done by making the individual literate, and bringing the individual in touch with the great literature and art and science of the age. Of course, this was possible (and necessary) only for the literate elite and those who could afford it and who could derive from it some sense of self-direction that opened up concrete alternatives.

Today, the situation is very different. Not only the literate elite but every individual lives in a rich cultural environment. The mass media and particularly television expose all individuals to every part of culture, the best as well as the worst, even if very different proportions. Liberation from unwitting dependence on *that* cultural environment requires that the analytical and critical skills derived from the study of the classics as well as from the lessons of social science be put to use in the everyday cultural environment. The development of those analytical critical skills and their application to television is the fresh approach to the liberal arts and a principal task of education today. Liberal education today is the liberation of the individual from the necessity of drifting with the swift cultural tides of our time and the preparation for such self-direction as may be necessary and possible. That is why I want to congratulate you for being in the vanguard of that great education movement and wish you luck.

Acknowledgments

The efforts of many individuals and organizations over a period of several years contributed to the success of the first national conference on the topic, *Children and Television: Implications for Education.* Administrators, teachers, children, and parents in schools in Eugene, Oregon; East Syracuse, New York; Idaho Falls, Idaho; Belpre, Ohio; and Las Vegas, Nevada, provided the opportunities for the early work in critical viewing skills that began in 1969. Their willingness to confront new problems and to be innovative in their programs was courageous in the late sixties when there was no national publicity or activity to be seen.

To Dr. George Gerbner must go the credit for proposing that a national conference on TV and children be held, and to Dr. Tom Payzant, then Superintendent of Schools in Eugene, Oregon, must go the credit for advancing the idea with us. Dr. Fritz Hess and Dr. Millard Pond, Superintendent in East Syracuse and Eugene in the late 60's, saw the need for educational responses to television, and offered encouragement and support in their schools.

The George Gund Foundation of Cleveland, Ohio, provided vital financial support to the Conference, and in a later grant, gave major support to the initial publication of Conference proceedings. Many other organizations and individuals gave time and thought as the Conference was planned and finally, carried out. The people who came from 35 states and 7 different nations to participate in the Conference were most critical to the success of this undertaking.

We intend that our efforts in making this unique publication available throughout the education community will be an expression of our gratitude to everyone who took part in this pioneer venture.

    Milton E. Ploghoft
    James A. Anderson
    Conference Directors

ANALYSIS AND REACTION SESSIONS DIRECTORS

Dr. Donald E. Agostino
Associate Professor
Indiana University
Media and Effects

Dr. James Betres
Associate Professor
Rhode Island College
Social Science Education

Dr. Charles Clift
Administrator
Broadcast Research Center
Ohio University
Media and Government

Dr. Thomas R. Donohue
Chairman
Department of Communication
University of Hartford
Media and Children

Dr. Aimee Dorr
Associate Professor
Annenberg School of Communications
University of Southern California
Children and Instruction Interventions

Dr. Robert Isaf
Associate Professor
SUNY - Cortland
Elementary Education

Dr. Albert Leep
Professor
Ohio University
Social Studies Curriculum

Dr. James T. Lull
Assistant Professor
University of California
Santa Barbara
The Family and Media

Dr. John Mallan
Associate Professor
Syracuse University
Teacher Education

Dr. Timothy P. Meyer
Associate Professor
University of Texas
Media and Children

Dr. James F. Parsley
Superintendent of Schools
Idaho Falls
Education Administration

Dr. Joe Rogus
Associate Professor
Cleveland State University
Administration and Instruction

Dr. Elizabeth Shipman
Assistant Professor
Coastal Carolina College
Education Supervision

Dr. Ellen Wartella
Research Assistant Professor
Communication Research Institute
University of Illinois
Children and Instructional Interventions

Dr. David Welton
Associate Professor
Texas Tech University
Social Science Education

CONFERENCE ADVISORY COMMITTEE

Dr. Donald Agostino
School of Communication
Indiana University
Bloomington, Indiana

Ms. Grace Baisinger
2870 Arizona Terrace N.W.
Washington, D.C. 20016
Past President, National Parent-Teacher Association

Mr. Jack Blessington
Director, Educational Relations
CBS Television Network
51 West 52 Street
New York, New York 10019

Ms. Peggy Charren, President
Action for Children's Television
46 Austin Street
Newtonville, Massachusetts 02160

Dr. Donald R. Frost
Assistant Superintendent for Administration
Community High School District 99
Administrative Service Center
1860 Sixty-Third Street
Downers Grove, Illinois 60515
Past President, Association for Supervision and
Curriculum Development

Ms. Susan Futterman, Manager
Children's Programs
American Broadcasting Company, Inc.
1330 Avenue of Americas
New York, New York 10019

Ms. Martha Gable
American Association of School Administrators
2601 Parkway, #845-C
Philadelphia, Pennsylvania 19130

Dr. George Gerbner, Dean
The Annenberg School of Communications
University of Pennsylvania
Philadelphia, Pennsylvania 19100

Ms. Sally Savage, Teacher of Reading
Member, Board of Directors
National Education Association
358 McDonald Avenue
McDonald, Ohio 44437

Ms. Pam Warford, Director
Community Relations
American Broadcasting Company, Inc.
1330 Avenue of the Americas
New York, New York 10019

Ms. Jeri E. Warrick-Crisman
Director of National Community Affairs
National Broadcasting Company
30 Rockefeller Plaza
New York, New York 10020

DATE DUE

APR 1 6			
DEC 1 2 '85			
DEC 1 9 '85			
FEB 2 6 '86			
NOV 2 9 '87			
DEC 21 1988			
NOV 2 7 1989			
NOV 2 0 2002			

GAYLORD · PRINTED IN U.S.A.